101 EASY-TO-DO AUTO REPAIRS

Other Books by Mort Schultz

*Repairing and Maintaining Yard Equipment
and Power Tools*

Car Care Q & A

*Fix It Yourself for Less: One Hundred Fifty
Money-Saving Repairs for Appliances and
Household Equipment*

Electronic Fuel Injection Repair Manual

What's Wrong with My Car?

*How to Install Dealer Options in Your
Own Car*

Wiring: Basic Repairs and Advanced Projects

*Modern Home Plumbing Repairs,
Improvements, and Projects*

101 EASY-TO-DO
AUTO REPAIRS

Mort Schultz

John Wiley & Sons, Inc.

New York • Chichester • Brisbane • Toronto • Singapore

Contents

Foreword

There are more than 100 repairs you can make to your car, pickup truck, van, or utility vehicle that require no mechanical knowledge, experience, or special tools. By doing them yourself, you can save hundreds, even thousands, of dollars in payments to professional mechanics.

According to automobile manufacturers, the repairs outlined in this book are those most commonly made to a vehicle over its lifetime. They are divided into two sections. Part I addresses engine performance problems. Part II deals with nonengine-related repairs. A table at the beginning of each section allows you to quickly locate the repair for your particular problem. Now, gather a few tools from your home workshop tool kit, roll up your sleeves, and follow the instructions. It's that simple.

Introduction

The 101 easy-to-do car repairs described in this book are remedies for the most commonly encountered automotive problems. Following the instructions will allow you to perform most or all of them yourself. You'll save hundreds if not thousands of dollars that you would otherwise hand over to a professional auto mechanic.

Every one of the repairs is simple. Most require only ordinary tools that you undoubtedly have in your home tool kit. A few require special inexpensive instruments that you may have to purchase. Before rushing out to buy an instrument, however, read the information carefully to determine whether it applies to your vehicle.

A list of the 101 repairs follows this introduction. The book is divided into two sections. Part I deals with repairs for engine-related problems; Part II with repairs for nonengine-related problems. A brief listing at the beginning of each part outlines those problems each repair is designed to fix. Match the problem you're having with your car to the applicable repair or repairs, and then go to work. You will probably notice that some of the nearly 200 photographs and illustrations in this book are of engines that were taken from cars and placed on stands. This was done to show the areas clearly. In this regard, I wish to acknowledge the cooperation of the Ford Motor Company Customer Service Division, New York District Office—specifically the photographic and technical support provided by Ford service engineers R. N. Bird, John J. Clark, and Bernie Golick.

Alphabetical Summary of Repairs by Component or System

(continued)

(continued)

(continued)

PART I
Engine Performance Problems

An engine that is performing poorly will transmit a distress signal that is hard to ignore. Signals have specific names and precise characteristics. To find a repair in this part of the book that may help you resolve an engine performance problem, identify the problem according to one of the following descriptions:

■ **DETONATION** (also called **AUTOIGNITION, PING,** and **SPARK KNOCK**) is a sharp, repetitive metallic rattle that is heard from the engine as you accelerate. The intensity of the noise varies with the load placed on the engine. The sound is least audible when the load is light, such as when you are accelerating smoothly to pass another vehicle. It is loudest when the engine is placed under a heavy load, such as when the car is climbing a steep hill or when you increase acceleration sharply.

■ **DIESELING** (also called **RUN-ON**) is the term used when an engine continues to run briefly after you turn off the ignition switch. The engine chugs for several seconds and usually emits an exhaust odor.

■ **HARD STARTING** is when the engine cranks briskly, but fails to start within 15 seconds. Hard starting and no-start (see below) are different problems.

■ **HESITATION** (also called **FLAT-SPOT ACCELERATION, SAG,** and **STUMBLE**) is a lack of response as you accelerate. The engine sags noticeably before taking off with a burst of energy.

■ **LOSS OF POWER** is when the engine provides less power than it once did.

■ **MISSING** (also called **MISFIRE**) is defined as a pulsation or jerking motion that is felt as you drive along at about 30 miles per hour or less. The sensation is often accompanied by a spitting sound from the exhaust.

■ **NO-START** is the term given to an engine that won't start. There are two variations: (1) an engine that won't crank and thus won't start, and (2) an engine that cranks normally but won't start.

■ **OIL LOSS,** a term that is self-descriptive, often points to serious problems and may signify a need to overhaul the engine. On the other hand, it may indicate a minor condition that you can easily resolve.

■ **OVERHEATING** is a buildup of engine temperature beyond the limits established by the manufacturer. It may or may not result from a loss of the engine cooling agent, called coolant.

■ **ROUGH IDLE** occurs when an engine runs unevenly or hops while idling.

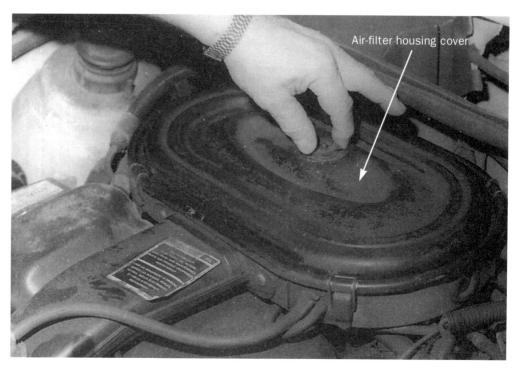

Air-filter housing cover

FIGURE 1
Most engines equipped with carburetors and throttle body fuel-injection systems have large housings that hold an air filter on top of the carburetor or throttle body.

■ **SURGING** describes a vehicle that can't seem to decide at which speed to run, alternately speeding up and slowing down even though you maintain a steady foot on the accelerator pedal.

An engine malfunction can cause more than one of these problems to occur simultaneously. Therefore, making a single repair may resolve a number of performance conditions that your car is experiencing.

To help make it easier for you to zero in on the proper repair, entries are organized alphabetically according to problem. A number of the repairs are not universal, but apply specifically to an engine possessing either a throttle body injection (TBI), multiport injection, or carburetor-equipped fuel system. Multiport injection is also called multipoint injection and port injection.

On the surface, TBI and carburetor-equipped fuel systems look alike. In these systems, either a carburetor or a throttle body sits on top of the engine. They are usually covered by a large housing that contains an air filter (Figure 1), or they have a long air duct extending from the carburetor or throttle body to an air-filter housing (Figure 2).

If your engine is equipped with a carburetor, you will see a choke plate when you look down the throat of the carburetor (Figure 3). A TBI fuel system has no choke. When you remove the air-filter housing and look down the throat of the throttle body, you will see one or two fuel injectors (Figure 4). If the engine has four cylinders, there will be one fuel injector. If

FIGURE 2
Some engines, such as this one with a TBI fuel system, have the filter housing remote from the throttle body. An air duct connects the throttle body with the housing.

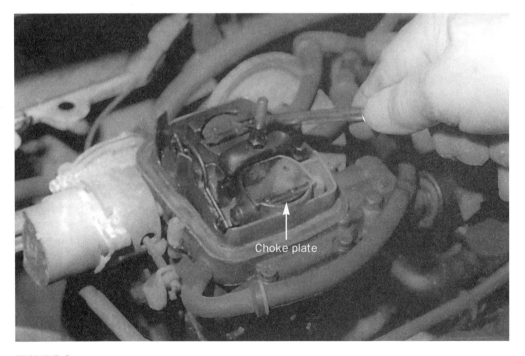

FIGURE 3
Carburetors have one, two, or four choke plates. This carburetor has two.

FIGURE 4
Throttle body fuel-injection systems have one or two fuel injectors.

FIGURE 5
Engines equipped with multiport fuel-injection systems are different in appearance from those with carburetors or TBI systems.

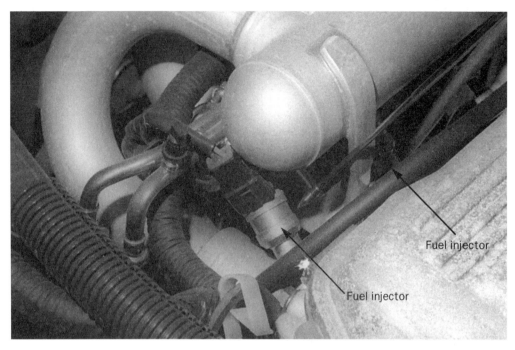

FIGURE 6
The presence of a fuel injector for each cylinder of the engine identifies a multiport fuel-injection system.

the engine has six or eight cylinders, there will be two fuel injectors.

The absence of a carburetor or its look-alike, a throttle body, means that the engine is equipped with a multiport injection system (Figure 5). With multiport fuel injection, a fuel injector screwed into the engine squirts gasoline into each cylinder (Figure 6). If a car has a six-cylinder engine and multiport injection, it has six fuel injectors. An eight-cylinder engine has eight fuel injectors.

Some repairs described in this section apply only to engines with carburetors, some to engines with carburetors or TBI, others to engines with TBI or multiport injection, and still others to all engines regardless of fuel system. The applicability of the repair to engine type is indicated by the heading to each entry. The following troubleshooting chart is a list of performance problems and their repairs described in this part of the book. This chart can be used as a guide to help you quickly locate a needed repair.

Problem	Repair	Page
Detonation	Use high-octane gasoline.	8
Detonation, dieseling, overheating	Clean radiator fins. Replace thermostat.	9 10

(continued)

5

(continued)

Problem	Repair	Page
Overheating	Apply a temporary repair for upper radiator hose.	95
Overheating at high speed only	Replace lower radiator hose.	98
Overheating	Replace defective hoses. Replace weakened coolant.	99 99
Overheating	Apply a temporary repair for radiator.	106
Overheating	Replace cooling-fan switch.	108
Overheating	Seal leaking head gasket.	111
Rough idle	Tighten loose carburetor or throttle body bolts. Replace defective carburetor or throttle body gasket.	112 112
Rough idle, stalling	Replace PCV valve, PCV hose, PCV dirt trap.	114
Rough idle, stalling	Service EVAP system.	120
Stalling in wet weather only	Service ignition or fuel system.	122

PROBLEM:	**Detonation**
REPAIR:	**Use high-octane gasoline**
ENGINES:	**All**

Run the engine on several tankfuls of a high-octane (92 or 93) gasoline to determine whether pinging (spark knock) subsides. As an engine gets older, its octane requirement increases. Switching to a higher-octane fuel may be all that is needed.

PROBLEMS: **Detonation, dieseling, overheating**

REPAIR: **Clean between radiator fins**

ENGINES: **All**

Radiator fins that become clogged with insects and other debris can increase engine temperature to the point where overheating in particular and possibly detonation or dieseling occur. If these problems are indeed being caused by dirty fins, the solution is simple.

Wait for the engine to get cold and then raise the hood. Using a soft bristle brush and a garden hose, clean debris from both sides of the radiator (Figure 7). If necessary, use an instrument with a pointed blade, such as an awl, to loosen stubborn residue embedded in the fins. Do this carefully to avoid damaging the radiator.

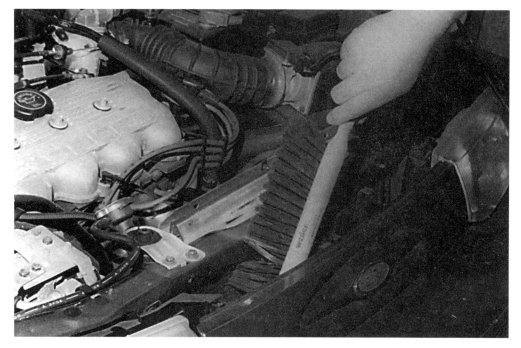

FIGURE 7
Sweeping the front and back sides of a radiator with a brush to clear away debris may resolve a performance problem caused by excessive heat. If debris is firmly embedded, try a forceful flow of water from a garden hose.

PROBLEMS: **Detonation, dieseling, overheating**

REPAIR: **Replace thermostat**

ENGINES: **All**

A cooling-system thermostat that sticks in a closed or partially closed position, preventing hot coolant from flowing through the radiator, will cause engine temperature to rise. If the thermostat sticks in the fully closed position, coolant will boil and the engine will overheat. If the thermostat sticks in a partially closed position, the engine may not overheat. However, excessive heat can cause the engine to detonate and/or diesel.

Here's how to replace the thermostat:

1. With the engine cold, place a clean pan under the radiator drain valve (petcock), remove the radiator cap, and open the valve to allow coolant to drain (Figure 8).
2. Discard used coolant in an environmentally safe way by pouring it into glass or plastic containers with screw-on caps. Label the containers "TOXIC LIQUID: AUTO COOLANT" and call your local environmental or recycling officials for disposal instructions.
3. Close the petcock.
4. Unscrew the bolts holding the thermostat housing together (Figures 9 and 10).
5. Before removing the thermostat, make a sketch that notes distinguishing marks on the thermostat and gasket and their positions relative to the housing (Figure 11). The sketch will help you install the new thermostat in the same way so as to prevent overheating.
6. Remove the thermostat and gasket from the housing (Figure 12). Discard the gasket, but keep the thermostat for the time being so you can take it to an auto parts store and buy a new one of the same type that is rated to open at the same temperature. Make sure a gasket comes with the new thermostat.
7. Use a wire brush to clean the thermostat housing and housing cover (Figure 13).
8. Following your sketch, install the new thermostat and gasket.
9. Position the thermostat housing and cover. Insert and tighten the bolts.
10. Install fresh coolant consisting of a 50:50 mixture of ethylene glycol antifreeze and water unless the ambient temperature in your region requires a stronger solution (see page 105).

FIGURE 8
To open the petcock at the bottom of the radiator, you may have to work under the car and maneuver pliers into a partially blocked space.

FIGURE 9
The location of the thermostat housing varies from car to car. Find it by tracing radiator hoses. Then, remove bolts to open the housing.

FIGURE 10
When the housing is open, you will be able to remove the thermostat.

11. Start the engine, let it run for a few minutes, turn it off, and check for a coolant leak around the thermostat housing. If coolant is leaking, further tighten the thermostat housing bolts.

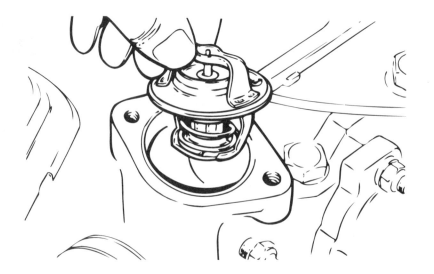

FIGURE 11
Some thermostats must be placed in a specific position to prevent overheating. As a precaution, make a sketch of the thermostat and any distinguishing characteristics, such as a vent hole, relative to their positions in the housing. This drawing illustrates a typical setup.

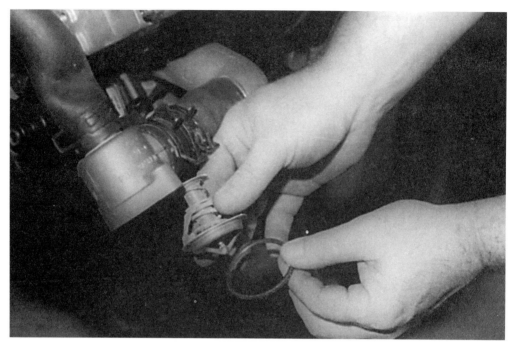

FIGURE 12
Remove the old thermostat and gasket by pulling them out of the housing.

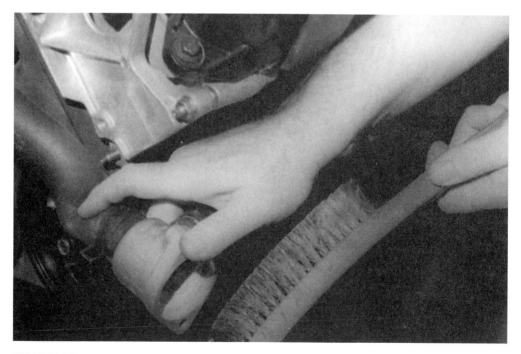

FIGURE 13
Make certain that the thermostat housing and cover are clean. Deposits on the surfaces can prevent proper sealing and cause a leak.

PROBLEMS: **Detonation, dieseling, hard starting**

REPAIR: **Treat engine with carbon solvent**

ENGINES: **All**

As an engine gets older, carbon that builds up in one or more of the combustion chambers (cylinders) can cause detonation, dieseling, and/or hard starting when the engine is warm. This repair may resolve these problems.

Buy a can of carbon solvent from an auto parts store or from the parts department of a new car dealer. One of the most effective solvents is GM Top Engine Cleaner™, which is sold by General Motors dealers. Following directions, pour solvent into the engine.

PROBLEMS: **Detonation, dieseling, hard starting, hesitation when accelerating, loss of power, missing, rough idle, stalling, surging**

REPAIR: **Replace damaged vacuum hose**

ENGINES: **All**

Vacuum is created inside an engine as pistons move up and down. It is transmitted to vacuum-operated components through hoses that are connected between each component and the engine (Figure 14). A cracked or loosened hose will result in a loss of vacuum, which can cause engine performance problems.

Here's how to find and repair a damaged vacuum hose:

If the performance problem started right after work was done on the engine, look for a kinked or pinched vacuum hose. Hoses must be straight or have only a slight curve to them. The emissions-control decal in the engine compartment usually has a diagram showing the location of vacuum components (Figure 15).

FIGURE 14
Hoses attached to components that use engine vacuum are cause for concern when a performance problem develops. In time, hoses can loosen or deteriorate.

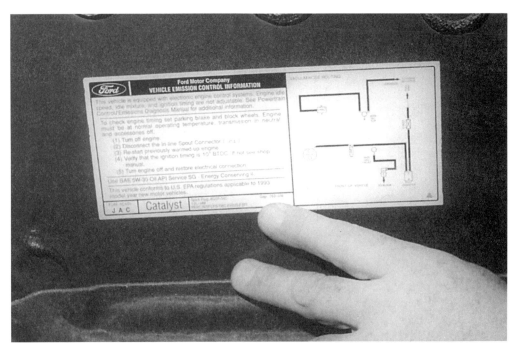

FIGURE 15
In addition to other data, the emissions-control information decal mounted in the engine compartment usually has a diagram showing vacuum-operated components and hoses.

Start the engine and let it idle. Then, using a four-foot length of $5/16$-inch vacuum hose (available from auto supply stores) as a stethoscope, hold one end to your ear and move the other end slowly across each vacuum hose (Figure 16). Vacuum escaping from a hole in the hose or from a loose connection will make a hissing sound.

CAUTION

As you do this test, keep away from belts and pulleys, and also from the cylinder head, which will get hot.

If the sound is loudest near a connection, turn off the engine, loosen the clamp, press the hose firmly onto the fitting, and retighten the clamp. Start the engine and again use your stethoscope to determine whether the hissing has stopped. If not, or if you hear the noise from somewhere else along the hose, turn off the engine, disconnect the hose at each end, buy a new hose (of the same diameter and length), and install it using new clamps (Figure 17).

FIGURE 16
Use a length of hose as a stethoscope to pinpoint a vacuum leak. You will hear a pronounced hissing sound from a damaged or loose hose.

FIGURE 17
When a defective vacuum hose has been identified, replace it by releasing the clamps at each end and pulling the hose off its fittings. Soak the ends of the new hose in hot water to soften them, making it easier to push them onto the fittings.

PROBLEMS: Detonation, dieseling, hard starting, missing

REPAIR: Replace worn spark plugs; determine whether plugs are correct type

ENGINES: All

Although the spark plugs currently in your car may be the type recommended in the owner's and service manuals, they may not be the best ones for your engine. There are at least three different types of plugs that will serve an engine; their difference lies in the length of their noses. Spark plugs with a longer nose retain heat for a longer time than plugs with a shorter nose.

Car manufacturers generally recommend spark plugs having an intermediate nose length. Such plugs are recommended for normal driving conditions—that is, an equal or almost equal combination of engine idling, slow-speed, and high-speed operation.

Sometimes reports sent to a manufacturer from the field indicate that the intermediate-nose spark plug is ineffective under normal driving conditions. The manufacturer will then issue an advisory to new car dealer service departments recommending that a switch be made to a plug with a longer or shorter nose. The engine performance problem you are experiencing may be a result of not having this up-to-date information.

A spark plug with a long nose is recommended if an engine is used mainly for stop-and-go and slow-speed driving. An engine that operates under these conditions has a tendency to build up carbon particles. The heat retained by the long nose of this type of spark plug burns off particles that accumulate on electrodes and that can keep the plug from firing.

Conversely, a spark plug with a short nose is recommended if an engine is used mainly for high-speed driving. Under this type of operation, spark plugs fire more often, which causes them to overheat, resulting in rapid electrode wear. The shorter nose dispels heat quickly to prevent this problem.

If your engine displays one of the performance problems noted above, jot down the designation of the plugs now in your engine. The designation is written on the upper insulator (Figure 18). To read the numerals, you will probably have to remove a plug from the engine (see below). Call the service department of a dealer who sells your make of vehicle and ask for verification that the plug designation is the one currently recommended by the manufacturer. If it is not, make the change.

Even if the designation is still valid, you may not be off the hook. The type of spark plug your engine needs depends on the type of driving

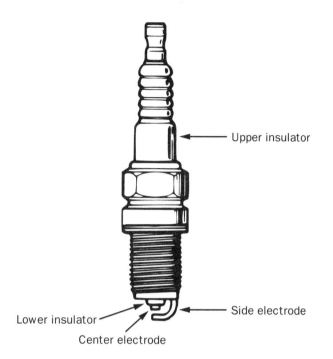

Upper insulator

Side electrode

Lower insulator

Center electrode

FIGURE 18
This drawing will
help you identify
the parts of a
spark plug referred
to in the text.

you do. Remove one or two plugs from the engine and examine the lower insulator, which is the ceramic part that surrounds the center electrode of the plug. If the insulator is coated with soot, plugs are being fouled by carbon. Switch to a hotter, or longer, plug. If the insulator is stark white, plugs are overheating. Switch to a colder, or shorter, plug.

In making the switch from hotter to colder or from colder to hotter, move up or down the heat-range scale one notch at a time. Replace each of the old spark plugs with new plugs that are all of the same designation. Drive the vehicle for several days to determine whether the performance problem has been solved.

Here is how to remove and install spark plugs, whether they are of the wrong type or are simply worn. Worn plugs will cause hard starting and missing.

CAUTION

To prevent injury and damage, perform this service when the engine is cold.

1. Grasp the boot of each spark plug cable. Twist and pull the boot to remove it from the plug (Figures 19 and 20).
2. Using an ear syringe, a piece of hose, or a drinking straw, blow dirt out of the spark plug ports to prevent particles from falling inside the engine as you remove the plugs. Particles can damage pistons and cylinder walls.
3. Using a spark-plug wrench or a socket wrench of the correct size, turn the plugs counterclockwise to remove them (Figures 21 and 22).
4. Notice whether the plugs have round or tapered seats (Figure 23). If round, they require seat gaskets. Spark plugs with tapered seats do not use gaskets.
5. Before installing new plugs, set the gap between electrodes to the specification given in your owner's manual or on the emissions-system information label mounted in the engine compartment (Figure 15). Slide a spark-plug feeler gauge of the correct size between the electrodes and move it from side to side (Figure 24). The electrode gap is set correctly when slight resistance is encountered as you move the gauge.

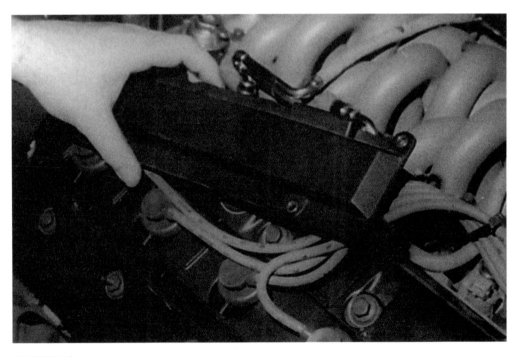

FIGURE 19
Spark plugs in many later-model engines are not visible. To get at the plugs, you may first have to unscrew and remove a cover.

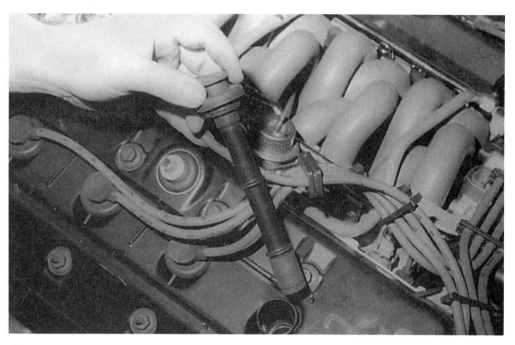

FIGURE 20
Plugs of some engines are buried deep inside the cylinder head and are fed current by cables that are connected to long transmitters. In the photograph, the cable and transmitter are visible; the plug is not. To remove the plug, first pull off the transmitter and cable.

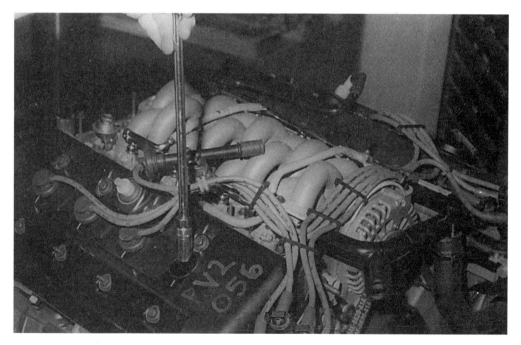

FIGURE 21
A long-handled socket wrench extension is needed to remove plugs from this engine.

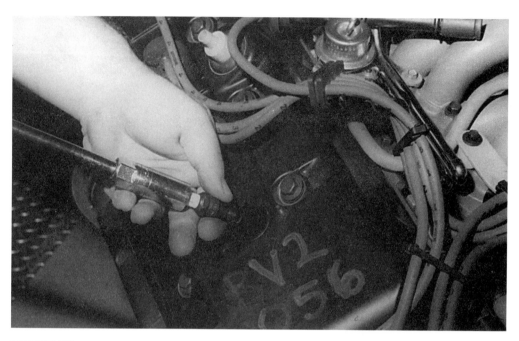

FIGURE 22
Grasp the plug with the socket and turn counterclockwise to remove the plug.

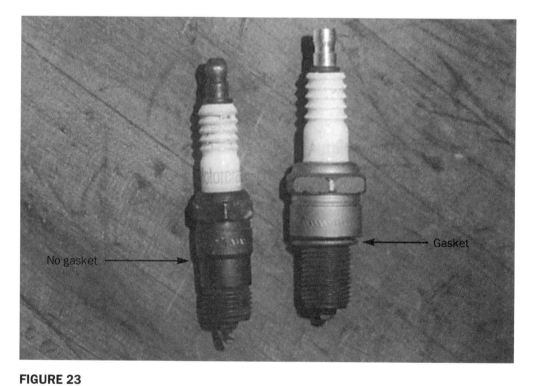

FIGURE 23
Spark plugs used in your engine may or may not have gaskets. The new plugs you install must be of the same type.

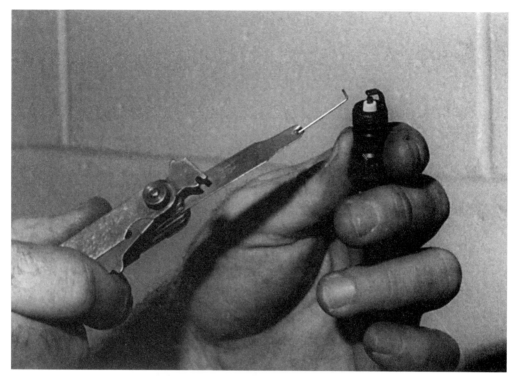

FIGURE 24
Check the spacing (gap) between electrodes with a spark-plug feeler gauge.

6. To adjust the gap, use the special bending tang that is part of the feeler gauge (Figure 25). Bend the side (hooked) electrode to widen or narrow the gap until the correct setting is obtained.

7. To install spark plugs, screw them into the engine until they tighten. Be careful not to cross threads.

8. Then, if your engine uses spark plugs that require gaskets, tighten them ¼ turn with a spark-plug or socket wrench. If the engine uses tapered-seat spark plugs, tighten them ¹⁄₁₆ of a turn with your wrench.

CAUTION

Plugs that are overtightened will be difficult to remove later on. This can result in stripping of the cylinder head, especially if the head is made of aluminum.

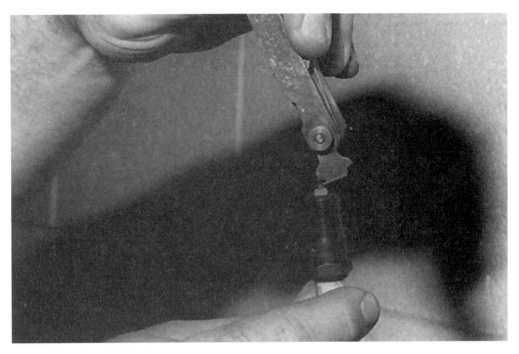

FIGURE 25
To adjust the electrode gap to specification, use the gapping tool that is part of the feeler gauge to bend the side electrode. Do not bend the center electrode or you will ruin the plug.

PROBLEMS: **Detonation, hesitation when accelerating, rough idle, stalling**

REPAIR: **Service heated air inlet system**

ENGINES: **Carburetor**

Most engines with carburetors have a heated-air inlet system integrated into the air-filter housing. This system is sometimes referred to as THER-MAC, an acronym for thermostatic air cleaner, or EFE, an acronym for early fuel evaporation. The system raises the temperature of air to about 105°F before the air mixes with gasoline in the carburetor. Warming of the fuel mixture cuts down on the amount of carbon monoxide that is expelled from the engine through the exhaust system. Carbon monoxide is an air pollutant. A heated-air inlet system consists of a valve plate, a vacuum diaphragm, and a heat-sensing switch (Figure 26). All are located in the air-filter housing. Each must function properly to maintain sound engine performance.

In most engines, the valve plate is inside the long nose (or snorkel) of the air-filter housing (Figure 27). The vacuum diaphragm is on top of

FIGURE 26
A long snout extending from the air-filter housing that has a "hump" (being pointed to here) indicates that your engine has a heated-air inlet system. The hump is the vacuum diaphragm, which is also called the vacuum motor.

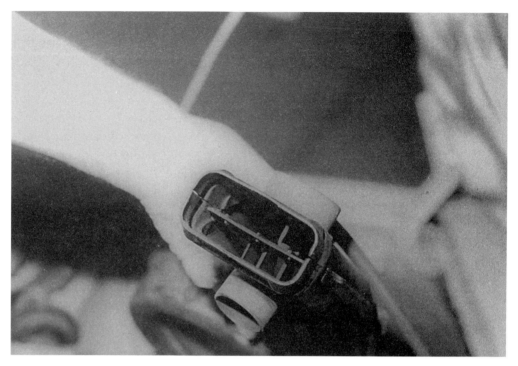

FIGURE 27
The valve plate inside the snorkel is the critical component. To be effective it must close and open properly relative to the temperature of the air.

the snorkel. The heat-sensing switch is inside the air-filter housing (Figure 28).

The vacuum diaphragm controls the closing and opening of the valve plate. The heat-sensing switch transmits "orders" to the diaphragm as to when the valve plate should be closed and opened.

The vacuum diaphragm works to keep the valve plate closed so it blocks the flow of air to the carburetor when the temperature of the air is less than 105°F. Instead, the air that the engine needs to run properly until it warms up is drawn into the carburetor from the exhaust manifold through an opening in the underside of the air-filter housing (Figure 29).

As the engine warms up and raises air temperature to above 105°F, the heat-sensing switch orders the vacuum diaphragm to release its hold on the valve plate. The plate opens to let air, now heated, reach the carburetor. When the plate drops, it falls over and seals the opening in the snorkel through which hot air from the exhaust manifold had been getting to the carburetor.

If the system isn't working right, the valve plate can stay open when it should close. This will allow cold air to enter the carburetor, causing the

FIGURE 28
The heat-sensing switch controls the functioning of the vacuum diaphragm. The vacuum diaphragm controls the closing and opening of the valve plate.

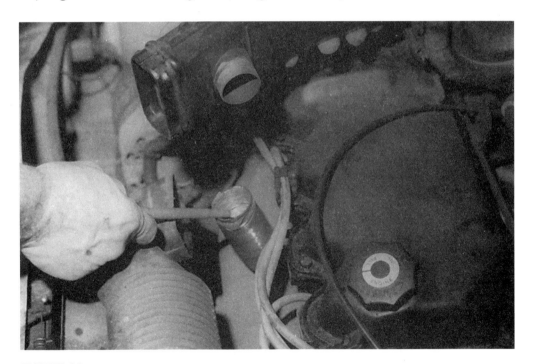

FIGURE 29
Heated air needed by an engine to run properly until it warms up is provided by the exhaust manifold through this duct, which should be inspected for damage if the engine performs poorly when it is cold.

engine to hesitate on acceleration and/or stall. Conversely, if the valve plate stays closed when it should open, the air from the exhaust manifold, which becomes increasingly hot as the engine warms up, will mix with gasoline. The mixture can get hot enough to start burning prematurely. This will result in detonation.

To determine whether one or more parts of a heated-air inlet system are causing a performance problem, wait for the engine to get cold and do this:

1. If the snorkel has a duct attached to its mouth, release the clamp and remove it (Figure 30).
2. Have an assistant start the engine as you shine a flashlight inside the snorkel to watch the valve plate.

CAUTION

Keep hands away from drive belts, pulleys, the cooling fan, and metal parts of the engine.

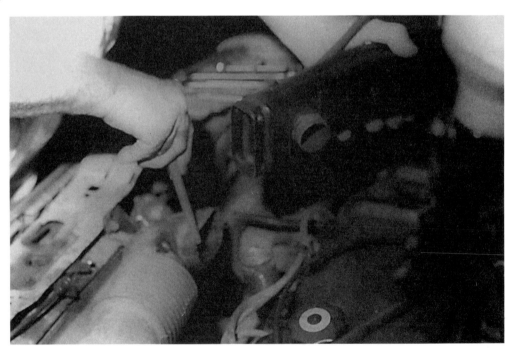

FIGURE 30
When the engine warms up and the valve plate opens, heated air from the engine compartment is delivered through this duct, which must be in good condition for the engine to run well.

As the engine starts, the valve plate should be closed over the throat of the snorkel. As the engine warms up, the valve plate should open. If neither of these things happens, one or more parts of the heated-air inlet system are malfunctioning. Here's what to do:

REPLACE THE AIR DUCT.   Poor engine performance will occur if one of the ducts transmitting air to the snorkel is damaged. Inspect ducts closely, especially inside the folds. If you find a hole or a split in a duct, release the clamp on each end, pull the duct free, and replace it with a new duct.

REPLACE THE VACUUM DIAPHRAGM.   With the engine turned off, remove and inspect the hose attached to the vacuum diaphragm. Replace a damaged hose (Figure 31).

Connect a hand-held vacuum tester pump to the hose fitting of the diaphragm and pump the handle until the meter records at least 10 inches of vacuum (Figure 32). If the meter needle begins to drop, indicating that the diaphragm is failing to retain vacuum, replace the air-filter housing or, if possible, replace the diaphragm this way:

1. Drill out the rivets holding the diaphragm to the snorkel (Figure 33).

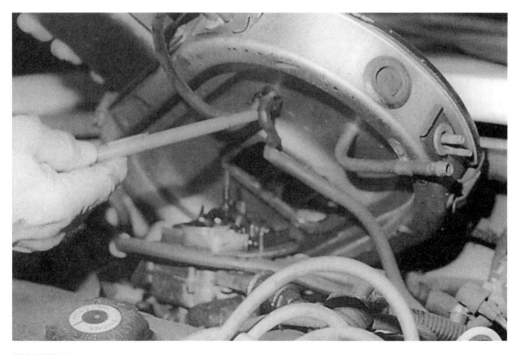

FIGURE 31
All hoses attached to the air-filter housing must be securely connected, straight, and undamaged.

Vacuum diaphragm

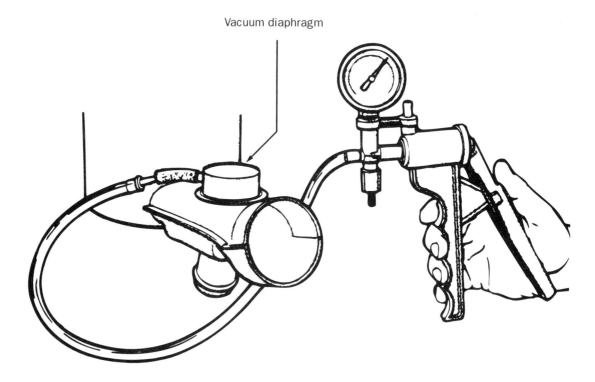

FIGURE 32
Test the vacuum diaphragm with a handheld vacuum tester. (Courtesy of Chrysler Corporation)

2. Lift the diaphragm off the snorkel and release the linkage that secures it to the valve plate.
3. Buy a new diaphragm from the parts department of a dealer who sells your make of vehicle. It should come with a retaining strap that you can wrap around the snorkel and secure with bolts.
4. Engage the linkage to connect the new diaphragm to the valve plate, place the diaphragm on the snorkel, and secure it with the retaining strap. Position the strap so it covers and seals the holes in the snorkel that were made when you drilled out the rivets.

REPLACE THE HEAT-SENSING SWITCH. If the ducts and vacuum diaphragm pass their tests, failure of the vacuum plate to function as it should probably lies with the heat-sensing switch. With the engine shut off, lift the air-filter housing off the carburetor and turn it over. In most heated-air inlet systems, two hoses are attached to the fittings of the heat-sensing switch (Figure 34). One hose connects to the vacuum diaphragm, the other to a fitting on the engine. Inspect hoses and replace them, if necessary.

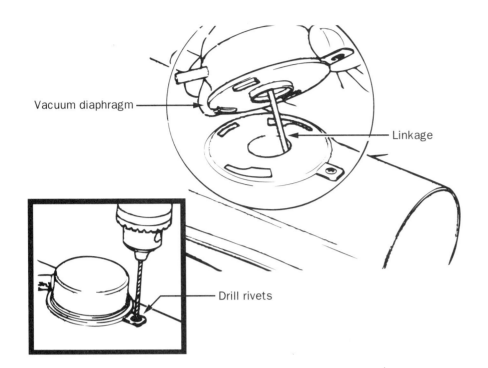

Vacuum diaphragm

Linkage

Drill rivets

FIGURE 33
If the vacuum diaphragm is riveted to the snorkel, you may be able to replace the part if you can obtain one from an auto parts distributor. The other alternative is to replace the air-filter housing. (Courtesy of Chrysler Corporation)

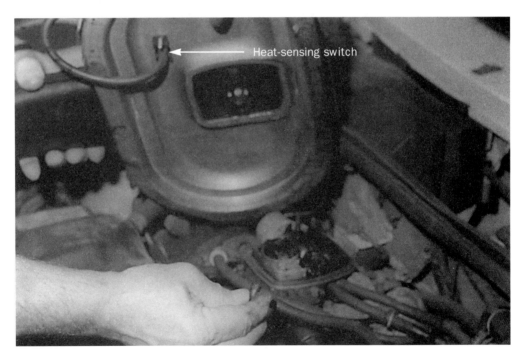

Heat-sensing switch

FIGURE 34
Hoses are the weakest components of a heated-air inlet system. The hose being held extends to a fitting on the engine and supplies the system with vacuum. The one attached to the underside of the air-filter housing provides vacuum for the vacuum diaphragm. Both are connected to the heat-sensing switch.

NOTE If one or more of the hoses are disconnected, this may be the reason for your problem. Attach hoses securely, make sure they run straight, reposition the air-filter housing on the carburetor, and redo the test described above to determine whether the valve plate now works as it should.

To replace a heat-sensing switch, use self-adhering labels to identify which hose is attached to which fitting of the switch. Pull hoses from the fittings. Release clips holding the switch to the air-filter housing (Figure 35). Turn the housing over and remove the switch.

Obtain a new heat-sensing switch of the same type from the parts department of a dealer who sells your make of vehicle. Position the new switch, secure it with the retaining clips, connect each hose to its correct fitting, and place the air-filter housing back on the carburetor.

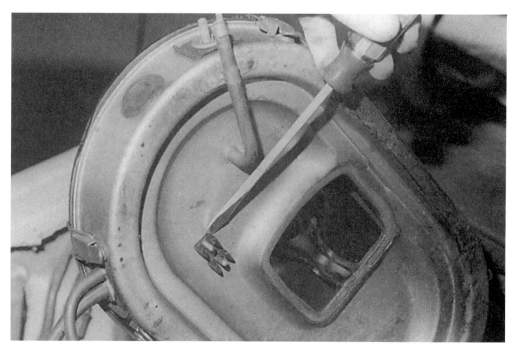

FIGURE 35
Replace the heat-sensing switch by prying off the retaining clip.

PROBLEMS:	Detonation, hesitation when accelerating, rough idle, stalling
REPAIR:	Replace EGR valve
ENGINES:	All

Most engines have an exhaust gas recirculation (EGR) valve to help prevent the formation of oxides of nitrogen (NOx). NOx in the presence of sunlight forms smog.

As fuel burns, temperature inside an engine can rise to a point at which it acts as a catalyst for nitrogen and oxygen molecules to fuse and form NOx. The EGR valve is used to divert exhaust gas to the cylinders. This gas, being relatively cool, keeps heat in the cylinders below the critical point at which fusion occurs.

A faulty EGR valve will introduce exhaust gas prematurely, diluting the strength of the fuel mixture in the cylinders. A lean fuel mixture degrades engine performance. Exhaust gas leaking into the cylinders causes an engine to idle rough and also causes one or more of the other performance problems listed above.

The weakest component of an EGR valve is an internal diaphragm that pulsates to meter exhaust gas to the cylinders. This rubberized part can develop a crack through which exhaust gas will enter the engine when it isn't supposed to. Here's how to determine whether this is what has happened and, if so, what to do about it:

Locate the EGR valve. It is usually under the carburetor or throttle body, on the intake manifold, or behind the air meter of an engine equipped with a multiport injection system (Figures 36 and 37). If you can't find the valve, ask a mechanic to point it out.

If the valve is raised high enough off the engine, make sure the engine is cold to avoid burning yourself and touch the bottom of the valve to establish whether its diaphragm is exposed (Figure 38). If the diaphragm is exposed, the bottom of the valve will feel soft and flexible. If the diaphragm is concealed, the bottom of the valve will be metal.

If your EGR valve has an exposed diaphragm, buy a spray can of carburetor solvent. Start the engine and let it idle. Obviously, the idle will be rough. If it wasn't, there would be no reason to suspect that the EGR valve was shot. Remember that the one performance problem that prevails with a faulty EGR valve is rough idle.

FIGURE 36
The EGR valve is usually easy to spot. This photograph shows the valve of an engine equipped with a throttle body fuel-injection system.

FIGURE 37
This photograph shows the EGR valve of an engine that has a multiport fuel-injection system.

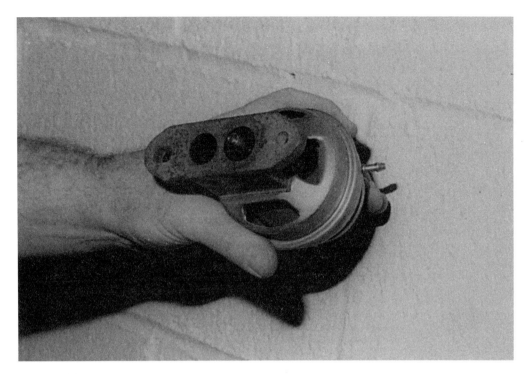

FIGURE 38
Some EGR valves have exposed diaphragms. Others don't.

Aim the can of solvent at the underside of the valve and spray the exposed diaphragm (Figure 39). If the diaphragm has a crack, the solvent will seal it and engine idle will become smooth, thus confirming that the EGR valve should be replaced.

CAUTION

Since this test is done with the engine running, keep away from drive belts, pulleys, and the cooling fan.

To test an EGR valve with a concealed diaphragm (Figure 40), follow these steps:

1. With the engine turned off, disconnect the hose from the EGR valve vacuum fitting (Figure 41).
2. Attach a hand-held vacuum analyzer to the fitting (Figure 42).

35

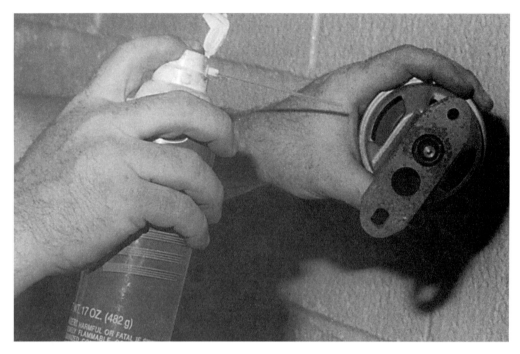

FIGURE 39
You can usually determine whether an EGR valve with an exposed diaphragm has failed by spraying the diaphragm with carburetor solvent while the engine is running.

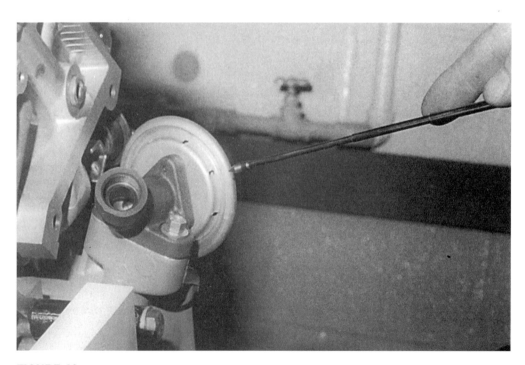

FIGURE 40
An EGR valve with an all-metal base that covers the diaphragm is tested using a hand-held vacuum analyzer.

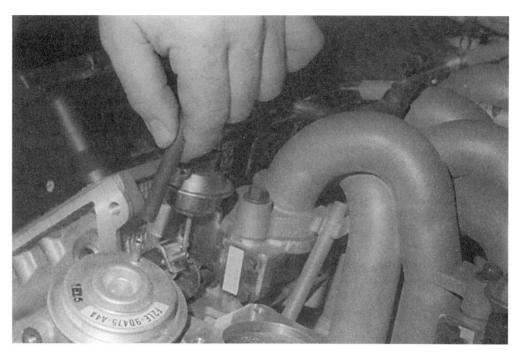

FIGURE 41
Begin testing an EGR valve that has a concealed diaphragm by pulling the hose off the fitting through which vacuum is fed to the valve from the engine. Inspect this hose for damage.

FIGURE 42
Attach a handheld vacuum analyzer to the EGR vacuum fitting.

3. Pump the handle of the vacuum analyzer until you encounter resistance and get a reading on the meter (Figure 43). Watch the meter for about 60 seconds. If the needle drops, the diaphragm is damaged. Replace the EGR valve.

> **NOTE** If you encounter no resistance and fail to get a reading, continue the procedure as outlined below. Some engines are equipped with a backpressure EGR valve. This type of valve operates by exhaust backpressure rather than vacuum and will not respond when vacuum is applied.

4. If your engine appears to be equipped with a backpressure EGR valve, remove the valve from the engine (Figure 44).
5. Place the base of the valve on a piece of cardboard and trace its outline to make a template.
6. Cut out the template and punch holes in it that coincide with the positions of the bolt holes in the valve.
7. Coat both sides of the template with chassis grease, which you can buy from an auto supply store.

FIGURE 43
Pump the handle of the vacuum analyzer until the needle no longer rises. If the needle falls back within 60 seconds, it indicates damage to the diaphragm. However, if pumping the handle results in no response from the needle (i.e., the needle stays on 0), you may be dealing with a backpressure EGR valve, which is tested as described in the text.

FIGURE 44
To remove an EGR valve, make sure that the engine is cold and undo the two bolts.

8. Place the template on the engine in the spot occupied by the EGR valve, put the EGR valve on top of the template, and bolt the valve and template to the engine (Figure 45).

IMPORTANT

Do *not* connect the vacuum hose to the EGR valve. Instead, press a golf tee or a screw into the opening of the hose to seal it.

9. Start the engine. Has rough idle disappeared? If so, the EGR valve is bad. Install a new one.

To replace a damaged EGR valve, make sure the engine is turned off. Remove the bolts holding the valve to the engine and take off the valve.

Stuff a rag into the hole left in the engine to prevent dirt from falling inside. Then, use a wire brush to clean around the hole (Figure 46). Remove the rag and install a new EGR valve, using a new gasket. Tighten bolts securely.

FIGURE 45
Test a backpressure EGR valve by positioning a cardboard template between the engine and the valve. Make sure bolts are tight to prevent a loss of vacuum.

FIGURE 46
Before installing a new EGR valve, it is important to clean the engine area to which the valve is bolted. Dirt particles may prevent the valve from seating securely.

IMPORTANT

Make sure the new EGR valve you buy is the correct one for your engine by taking the old valve and your vehicle identification number (VIN) to an auto supply store or to the parts department of a new car dealership that sells your make of vehicle. The VIN is printed on registration and proof-of-insurance documents. It is also embossed on a plate that is mounted on the corner of the dash on the driver side of the vehicle (Figure 47).

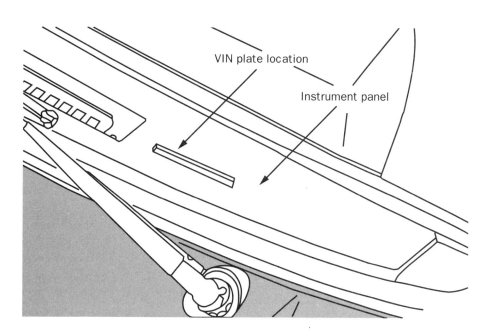

VIN plate location

Instrument panel

FIGURE 47
The vehicle identification number is located on the corner of the instrument (dash) panel on the driver side. It can be seen by looking into the vehicle through the windshield. (Courtesy of Chrysler Corporation)

PROBLEM: **Dieseling**

REPAIR: **Alter engine shut-off procedure**

ENGINES: **All**

An engine that continues to run for a brief time after you turn off the ignition switch will not sustain damage. However, the experience can be disconcerting. Here's a simple way to prevent dieseling until you find time to check for possible causes and make a permanent repair:

When you bring the vehicle to a halt, hold your foot firmly on the brake pedal. Keep an automatic transmission in Drive as you turn off the ignition switch.

To turn off an engine in a vehicle that has a manual transmission, bring the car to a stop. Your left foot should be depressing the clutch pedal, your right foot should remain firmly on the brake pedal, and the transmission shift lever should be in gear. Do not turn off the ignition key. Instead, stall the engine by letting up on the clutch pedal.

PROBLEM: **Hard starting in cold weather**

REPAIR: **Clean automatic choke**

ENGINE: **Carburetor**

The automatic choke plate of an engine equipped with a carburetor must function properly if the engine is to start promptly in cold weather. An indication that dirt is impeding the operation of the choke plate is when the engine starts promptly in warm weather, but fails to start within 15 seconds in cold weather. Here's what to do:

1. With the engine cold, remove the air-filter housing from over the carburetor so you can watch how the choke plate is functioning (Figure 48).
2. Have an assistant press the accelerator pedal to the floor and release it. The choke plate should close over the carburetor throat.
3. Have the assistant crank the engine. When the engine starts, the choke plate should immediately crack open and continue to open gradually as the engine runs. It should be wide open within one minute.

If the choke plate doesn't work this way, something is wrong with the choke system. The heating element may have burned out, a vacuum-operated mechanism called the choke break may be damaged, or the spring that controls choke movement may have to be replaced. These repairs are best handled by a mechanic. First, however, try the following easy-to-do repair, which frequently solves the problem:

1. Buy a can of carburetor and choke cleaning solvent from an auto supply store.
2. Spray solvent on the choke-plate pivot points and on the link attached to the choke plate (Figures 49 and 50).
3. Use a toothbrush to scrub off dirt.
4. Wipe the plate and the link dry.

FIGURE 48
To observe the choke plate or plates, open the air-filter housing cover and remove the air filter. Depending on the type of carburetor, there will be one, two, or four choke plates.

FIGURE 49
If choke plate movement is being hampered by dirt, treatment with carburetor and choke cleaner should resolve the problem.

FIGURE 50
This drawing illustrates the spots at which to concentrate carburetor and choke cleaner. (Courtesy of Chrysler Corporation)

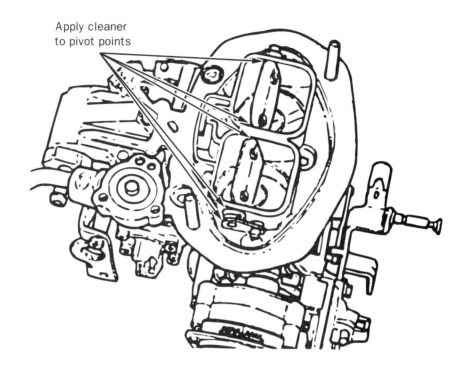

Apply cleaner
to pivot points

PROBLEM: **Hard starting in warm weather**

REPAIR: **Have leaking fuel injector replaced**

ENGINE: **TBI**

> **NOTE** The repair cited for this problem, replacing a faulty fuel injector, should be left to a professional mechanic. That's because a fuel-injection system is pressurized. Relieving pressure so a faulty injector can be replaced usually requires special equipment. However, the inspection procedure to ascertain whether a fuel injector actually requires replacement is easy to do and within the capability of most vehicle owners. Unfortunately, many mechanics do not take time to establish without doubt whether a fuel injector is to blame for the problem noted above. They assume this is the case and proceed to replace the injector, which often is not causing the condition. The outcome: The vehicle owner pays for an expensive job but is left with the same performance problem.

Throttle body fuel-injection systems have fuel injectors that can be inspected to determine whether they are leaking. If gasoline drips from an injector, the engine will flood and will be hard to start, especially in warm weather.

To find out whether a leaking fuel injector in an engine equipped with a TBI fuel system is causing a problem, do the following:

1. Remove the air-filter housing.
2. Start the engine and let it warm up. Then, turn it off.
3. Watch the tip of the fuel injector for 15 minutes to see whether any gasoline drips (Figure 51). Even one drop is too much.

> **NOTE** The throttle bodies of six- and eight-cylinder engines have two fuel injectors. Both must be observed for 15 minutes.

If you see a drop of gasoline, the faulty fuel injector should be replaced.

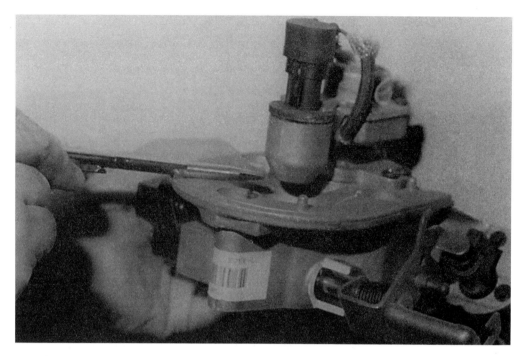

FIGURE 51
This photograph illustrates the fuel injector of a TBI fuel system. A defect can cause
fuel to drip from the injector and flood the engine. This will result in hard starting,
especially in warm weather.

PROBLEMS: **Hard starting, hesitation when accelerating, loss of power, rough idle**

REPAIR: **Replace air duct**

ENGINES: **All**

The innocent-looking accordion-fold duct through which air flows into the fuel system should be closely scrutinized if one of the problems listed above occurs (Figure 52). One or two ducts are connected to the air-filter housing of a vehicle equipped with a carburetor or TBI fuel system. If your engine has a multiport fuel-injection system, an air duct is attached to the air intake.

When an air duct splits or cracks, excess air introduced into the fuel system dilutes the fuel mixture. Forced to run on an overly lean mixture, the engine falters and performs poorly. To determine whether this is the problem with your engine, inspect each air duct for split or cracked areas by spreading apart every fold (Figure 53). Replace a damaged duct.

Each end of a duct is held by a clamp. To remove the duct, loosen the clamps and pull the duct free (Figures 54 and 55).

FIGURE 52
The innocent-looking rubber duct that transports air to the fuel system is one of the more sinister parts of an engine. Any crack or hole that develops, no matter how small, allows excessive air into the system, which will cause a performance problem.

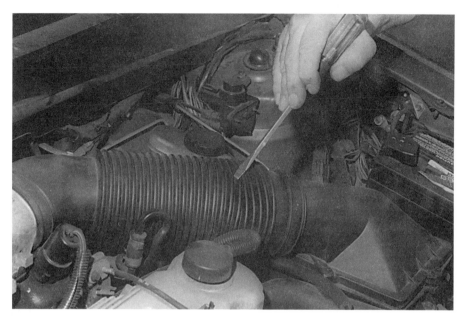

FIGURE 53
To check for damage, draw apart each fold and inspect the entire circumference.

After attaching a new duct, tighten the clamps, but not excessively. A clamp that is overtightened can cut the duct. Turn clamp screws until you can no longer tighten them without applying force. Then, turn them just ¼ turn more.

FIGURE 54
To replace a damaged air duct, loosen the clamps.

FIGURE 55
Pull the damaged air duct free and remove it.

PROBLEMS: **Hard starting, missing, no-start, rough idle**

REPAIR: **Replace spark plug cables; replace distributor cap**

ENGINES: **All**

Cables act as highways through which electricity flows to the spark plugs. In time, they can fail. When they do, voltage needed by spark plugs to ignite the fuel mixture won't reach the plugs, resulting in hard starting, missing, and/or rough idle. If the problem is severe, the engine won't start.

As time passes, the integrity of the distributor cap can also be compromised. The distributor cap contains metal pickup terminals that parcel current to spark plug cables (Figure 56). When one or more of these fail, the result is the same as with faulty spark cables.

A distributor cap can also crack, allowing moisture into the distributor, where it can suppress the production of electricity. The result will be an engine that won't start when it is raining or snowing, or when the relative humidity is high.

FIGURE 56
This photograph illustrates the inside of a distributor cap. The metal pickups, which transmit high voltage to spark plugs through cables, may erode or the cap may crack. Either condition will result in poor engine performance.

Follow this procedure to replace spark plug cables and the distributor cap:

CAUTION

Make sure the engine is cold.

---

1. On self-adhering labels, write consecutive numbers that correspond to the number of cylinders in your engine. Make two sets. For example, if your engine has four cylinders, you should have two labels marked "1," two labels marked "2," two labels marked "3," and two labels marked "4."

2. Look to see whether the ignition system uses an external ignition coil (Figures 57 and 58). If so, a cable will extend from the ignition coil to the distributor cap. It, too, should be replaced.

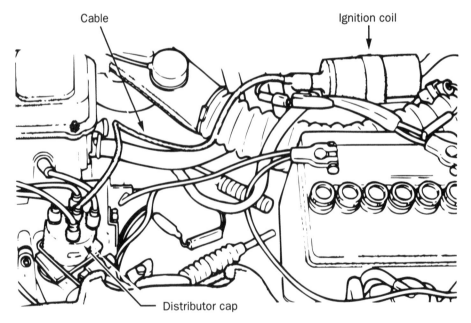

FIGURE 57
In addition to cables that extend to spark plugs, the cable between the distributor cap and the external ignition coil should be inspected. It, too, can go bad. (Courtesy of Chrysler Corporation)

FIGURE 58
The cable that extends to an external ignition coil is always the cable that attaches to the center post of the distributor cap.

3. Buy a replacement set of cables and a new distributor cap from an auto parts supplier.

4. Stick the first label marked with a "1" on one of the cables (Figure 59). Trace the cable to where it connects to the distributor and place the other label marked "1" on the distributor tower. Follow the same procedure to identify the other cables with their respective towers.

5. Align the new distributor cap with the old one so that distinguishing features and markings on the caps coincide. Then, unlatch the old cap. Some types are held by screws, others by clamps. Turn the screws to release the cap (Figure 60). If the cap is held by clamps, place a screwdriver between the backside of the clamp and the distributor housing and pry against the clamp until it snaps open. Remove the old cap and install the new one in exactly the same position.

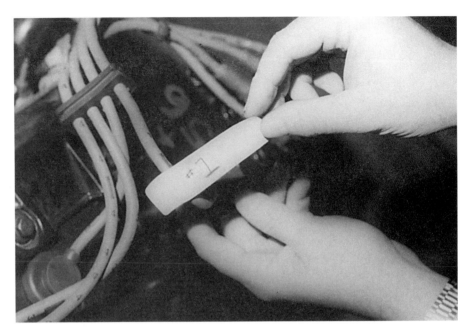

FIGURE 59
When disconnecting cables or hoses, be sure to identify which cable or hose goes where. Reconnecting a cable or hose incorrectly will result in crossfire.

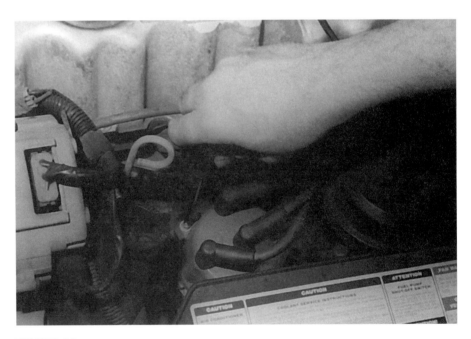

FIGURE 60
Most distributor caps are held to the distributor by screws. To release the cap, turn the screws.

6. From the new set of cables, select the one that most closely matches the length of the cable marked "1" on the engine. Disconnect that cable from the spark plug and replace it with the new cable. Make sure the new cable is routed to the new distributor cap exactly like the old one. Push the cable into the same slot in the cable holder that the old cable occupied (Figure 61). Attach the cable securely to the spark plug and the distributor. Follow this procedure until all cables have been replaced.

7. When you are finished, inspect the setup to make sure cables crisscross (Figure 62). They should not be parallel to one another, or a condition called engine crossfire will result. Crossfire occurs when a cable serving a cylinder draws current from a cable serving another cylinder because the two cables run parallel and close to each other. The spark plug with the induced current can then fire prematurely, which will damage parts in the cylinder. If cables are parallel, disconnect and cross them.

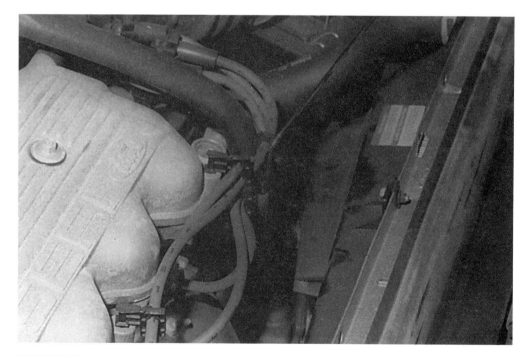

FIGURE 61
Make sure each new cable snaps into the same slot that the old cable occupied in the cable holder.

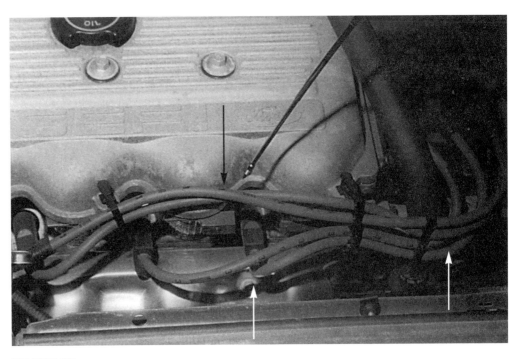

FIGURE 62
Make sure cables crisscross (arrows). If they don't, a condition called crossfire will occur, with possibly devastating results to the engine.

PROBLEMS: **Hard starting, missing, no-start, rough idle, stalling, surging**

REPAIR: **Repair fuel injector wire**

ENGINES: **TBI and multiport injection systems**

Fuel injectors are electrically operated solenoid valves that spray gasoline into cylinders of an engine that is equipped with a throttle body or multiport fuel-injection system (Figure 63). If an injector doesn't receive electricity because of a damaged wire, it will not operate and gasoline will not reach a particular cylinder.

Most owners of vehicles with fuel-injection systems can determine whether this problem is causing one of the performance conditions listed above by using an instrument called an EFI-LITE (or NOID-LITE) (Figures 64 and 65). You can buy the particular design of EFI-LITE that fits the shape of the connectors used by your fuel system from an auto parts store or directly from one of the companies listed on page 59. The instrument costs less than $10.

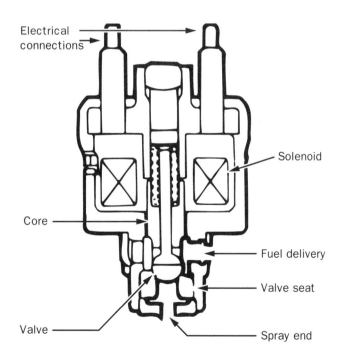

Electrical connections

Solenoid

Core

Fuel delivery

Valve seat

Valve

Spray end

FIGURE 63
Although they look different, fuel injectors of throttle body systems (illustrated) and those of multiport systems work the same way. Fuel is delivered to the injector. When the injector receives an electrical charge, the solenoid opens the valve, allowing fuel to spray into the engine. An electrical disruption will prevent this from happening. (Courtesy of General Motors)

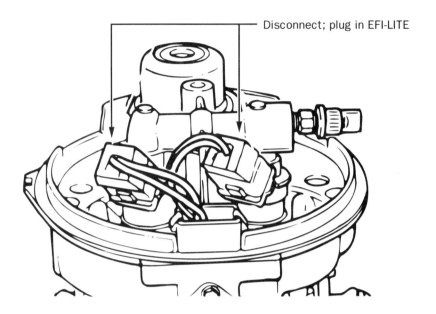

Disconnect; plug in EFI-LITE

FIGURE 64
Whether your vehicle has a throttle body or a multiport fuel-injection system, determining whether there is an electrical disruption to one or more of the fuel injectors is done by disconnecting the electrical connector from the injector. This drawing illustrates a TBI system with two fuel injectors.

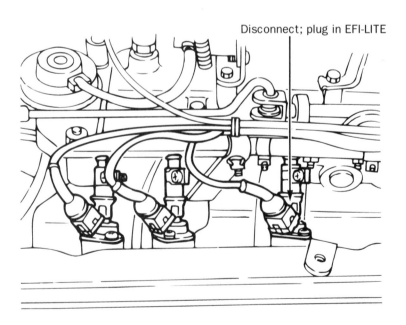

Disconnect; plug in EFI-LITE

FIGURE 65
This drawing illustrates three of the six fuel injectors of a multiport system on a six-cylinder engine.

The following companies sell EFI-LITE:

- Borroughs Tool Company, 2429 North Burdick Street, Kalamazoo, MI 49007; 800-253-0138
- Kent-Moore Tool Company, 29784 Little Neck, Roseville, MI 48066; 800-345-2233
- OTC, 2013 4th Street NW, Owatonna, MN 55060; 800-533-5338

Here is how to use an EFI-LITE to uncover a disruption in electricity to fuel injectors:

1. With the engine turned off, pull apart the connectors that join the electricity-delivery wire to one of the fuel injectors (Figures 66 and 67).

   > **NOTE** If you are working on a TBI system, you must first remove the air-filter housing.

2. Plug the EFI-LITE into the connector to which the wire is attached.

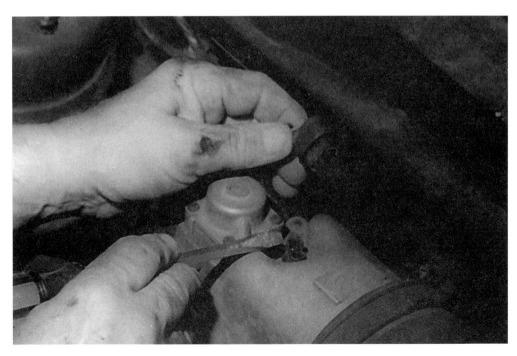

FIGURE 66
To disconnect the electrical connector from the fuel injector of a TBI system, simply pull the connector off the injector.

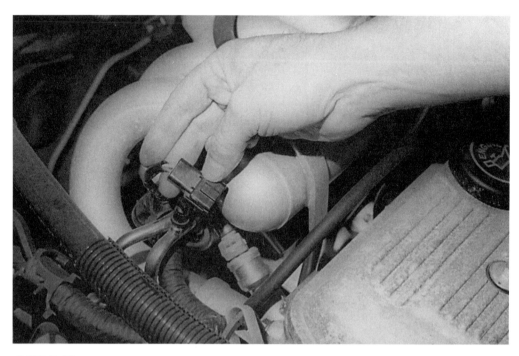

FIGURE 67
To disconnect the electrical connectors from the fuel injectors of a multiport system, simply pull the connector off each injector.

3. Have an assistant crank the engine as you watch the EFI-LITE. If the light gives off a pulsating glow, the electrical system is working properly. Reattach the wire to the fuel injector and test the next injector.

If the EFI-LITE does not glow, or if the beam it emits doesn't pulsate, the reason is often a short circuit caused by a bare wire in contact with a metal part of the engine. Examine the wire leading to the fuel injector to determine whether insulation has been rubbed off so that the wire is protruding. If a bare wire exists, wrap it with electrician's tape, which is available from hardware stores, to make the repair.

PROBLEMS:	**Hesitation when accelerating, rough idle**
REPAIR:	**Replace fuel filter**
ENGINE:	**Carburetor**

The fuel system of an engine equipped with a carburetor uses one of three types of filters to trap contaminating material that may be present in gasoline because of dirt in the vehicle fuel tank or dirt in the tanks of gasoline stations. Dirt that enters the carburetor can block passages, impeding the flow of fuel to the engine and resulting in poor engine performance.

The three types of fuel filters have the following characteristics:

- One type of filter, which is completely visible, is connected to and is part of the fuel line. This is called an in-line fuel filter.
- Another type of filter, also visible, is screwed into the carburetor inlet. This is also called an in-line fuel filter.
- The third type of fuel filter is inside the carburetor inlet. This is called an internal fuel filter.

If a fuel filter has not been replaced for some time in an engine that hesitates on acceleration and/or idles rough, replacing it now may solve the problem. Here is how to do this job for each of the three types of filters:

In-Line Filter #1

1. With the engine cold, place a rag under the fuel filter to catch gasoline that may drip as you remove the part.
2. Using pliers or a screwdriver, release the clamps (Figure 68).
3. Pull hoses from the fuel line to release the filter.
4. Note the arrow on the new fuel filter that shows the direction of fuel flow. Place the filter in position with the arrow pointing toward the carburetor.
5. Attach hoses to the fuel line and slide clamps in place to secure the filter to the fuel line.
6. Remove the rag and start the engine. With the engine running at idle, check around filter hoses to make sure that no gasoline is leaking.

In-Line Filter #2

1. Stuff a rag under the filter to catch gasoline that may drip.
2. Remove the air-filter housing from the carburetor.

FIGURE 68
The in-line fuel filter that is completely visible is the easiest of the three types of filters to replace.

3. Unscrew the fuel line from the fuel filter (Figure 69).
4. Unscrew the filter from the carburetor.
5. Screw in and tighten the new filter, attach the fuel line, remove the rag, start the engine, and check to make sure that no gasoline is dripping.

Internal Filter

1. Stuff a rag under the fuel line at the carburetor inlet to catch gasoline that may drip.
2. Remove the air-filter housing from the carburetor.
3. Unscrew the fuel line from the carburetor inlet.
4. Unscrew the large nut that holds the filter inside the carburetor inlet (Figure 70). The filter, which is equipped with a spring, will pop out. Discard the filter, but hold onto the spring. New fuel filters usually don't come with new springs.
5. Insert the new filter into the carburetor inlet so that it presses against the spring.

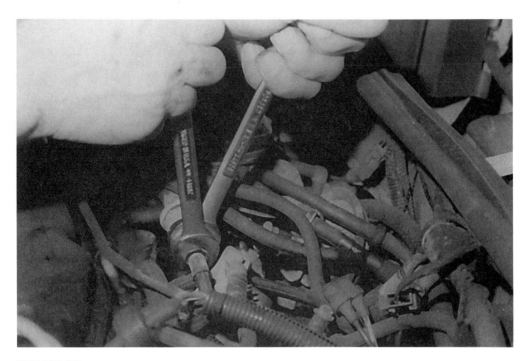

FIGURE 69

This photograph shows how to remove the type of in-line fuel filter that is screwed into, but protrudes from, the carburetor inlet. Note that two wrenches are used to unscrew the fuel line from the fuel filter to prevent distortion of the fuel line. One wrench holds the line steady, while the other is turned. Always use this double-wrench technique to disconnect and reconnect a fuel line.

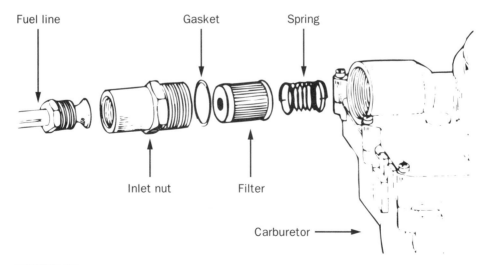

FIGURE 70

This drawing identifies the parts of an internal fuel-filter assembly. Remember to use double-wrenching (see Figure 69) to unscrew the fuel line from the fuel inlet retaining nut. (Courtesy of General Motors)

6. Screw on the large retaining nut. Turn the nut as far as you can by hand, then tighten it with a wrench.

7. Attach and secure the fuel line, remove the rag, and start the engine. With the engine running at idle, check around the fuel line to make sure that no gasoline is leaking.

PROBLEMS: **Hesitation when accelerating, surging**

REPAIR: **Service oxygen sensor**

ENGINES: **All**

Engines equipped with electronic control systems, which are usually referred to erroneously as computerized systems, have oxygen (O_2) sensors that monitor the oxygen content of the exhaust. This includes all engines with throttle body and multiport fuel injection systems and some engines with carburetors.

The oxygen sensor allows a microprocessor to adjust the fuel system according to the conditions under which the engine is operating. The fuel system is thus able to adjust itself to deliver a leaner or richer mixture as engine operating conditions require. If the sensor malfunctions, the engine will run on a leaner fuel mixture when it needs a richer mixture or vice versa. Hesitation on acceleration and/or surging will result.

That part of an electronic engine control system involving the oxygen sensor does not begin to function until the engine is warm. Therefore, if hesitation and/or surging occurs immediately after a cold engine is started, the fault does not lie with the sensor. It is only when one or both of these performance problems occur a few minutes after the engine has been running that the sensor becomes suspect.

There is another clue to suggest that an oxygen sensor is malfunctioning: The CHECK ENGINE light on the dash glows.

Before consulting a mechanic, you may want to do the tests described here. One of them may straighten out the problem. If it does, you can replace the sensor yourself.

Begin by locating the oxygen sensor. With most engines, it is on the exhaust manifold and is accessible from under the hood (Figure 71). With other engines, the oxygen sensor is tapped into some other part of the exhaust system. Getting at it can only be done from under the car.

With the engine cold, pull the electrical wire connector from the sensor (Figure 72). Wipe the insides of both halves of the connector, and then press the two halves firmly together. Check engine performance. If it is better, the cause of the performance problem was simply a dirty oxygen sensor connection. No further service is necessary.

If cleaning the connector doesn't help, disconnect the connector again. Use a wrench to remove the sensor from the engine (Figure 73). If the sensor binds in the engine, squirt penetrating oil around the sensor and wait at least 15 minutes. Then, start the engine and let it run for about five minutes before trying to unscrew the sensor with a wrench.

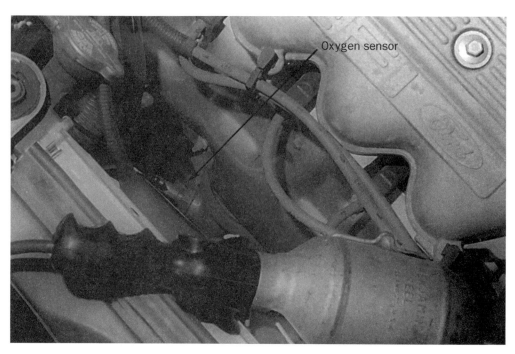

Oxygen sensor

FIGURE 71
Although it is buried in the recesses of an engine compartment, the oxygen sensor can usually be reached for servicing without too much trouble.

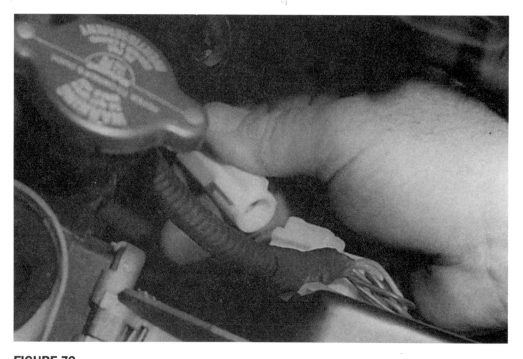

FIGURE 72
The first step in servicing the oxygen sensor is to trace the wire emanating from it until you come to a connector. Then, pull the connector apart. Make sure the engine is cold.

CAUTION

Be very careful. The engine will be red hot. Wear heavy gloves in case your hand slips.

When you finally have the sensor out of the engine, you will probably find oil, grease, or particles clogging the air-intake ports (Figure 74). The sensor may instead be contaminated with carbon, silicon, or lead. In either case, replace the sensor.

Carbon (black, sooty) contamination is caused by an overrich fuel mixture, which indicates a fuel system malfunction. Consult a mechanic, who should troubleshoot the fuel system to find and correct the problem.

Silicone (brownish) contamination is the result of a compound having been used on the engine—usually RTV (room-temperature vulcanizing) gasket material or a spray containing silicone. Avoid this in the future.

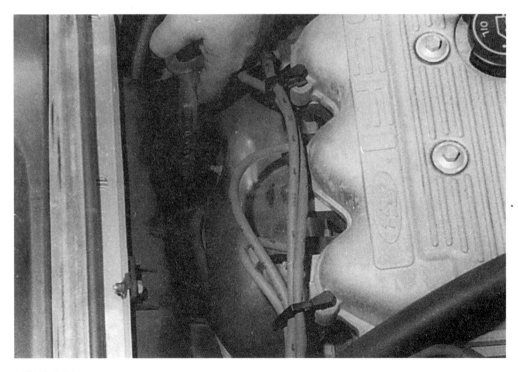

FIGURE 73
Reach down with a wrench, engage the oxygen sensor, and loosen it. You can then unscrew it by hand, but make sure the engine is cold.

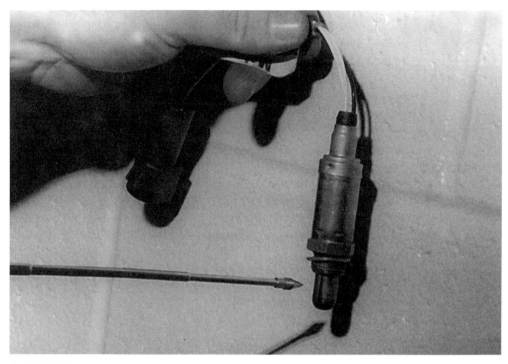

FIGURE 74
Examination of the intake ports of an oxygen sensor will often reveal the cause of failure.

Lead (silvery) deposits result from the use of leaded gasoline when the engine requires unleaded gasoline. This must be avoided to prevent serious damage to parts of the emissions-control system.

To install a new oxygen sensor, buy the correct one for your engine by giving the vehicle identification number to an auto parts supplier or to the parts department of a dealer who sells your make of car. Ask parts personnel whether the new sensor possesses a coating of high-temperature antiseize compound on its threads. If not, buy a tube of compound and coat the threads yourself (Figure 75). This should also be done when re-installing a sensor you removed from the engine for examination.

With the engine cold, thread the new sensor into the engine, being careful to avoid crossing threads. Tighten the sensor, but don't ram it down. Turn the sensor with a wrench until you encounter resistance. Then, turn it just ½ turn more.

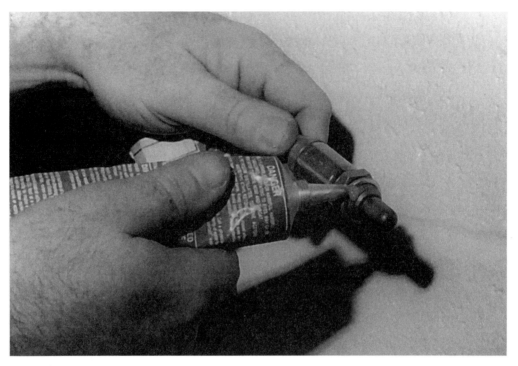

FIGURE 75
Coating the threads of an oxygen sensor with a high-temperature antiseize compound will prevent it from seizing in the engine. This will ease its removal if you ever again have to replace it.

PROBLEM: **Loss of power**

REPAIR: **Replace air filter**

ENGINES: **All**

The air filter traps dirt to prevent it from being carried into the fuel system along with air. A dirty air filter causes an engine to run on an overabundance of gasoline, a condition that results in reduced power output. The life expectancy of an air filter in your vehicle will depend on the quality of the air in the region where you drive.

Air filters of engines with carburetors and throttle body fuel-injection systems can be found in a housing that sits on top of the carburetor or the throttle body, or in a housing that is connected to the carburetor or throttle body by an air duct (Figure 76). Remove the cover over the housing by releasing the screws, wing nuts, or clips (Figure 77). Take the filter out of the housing and hold it to the light (Figure 78). If it is dirty, buy a new filter of the same type, place it in the housing, and reattach the cover.

Servicing the air filter of an engine that has a multiport fuel-injection system may be somewhat more complicated, only because the air-filter

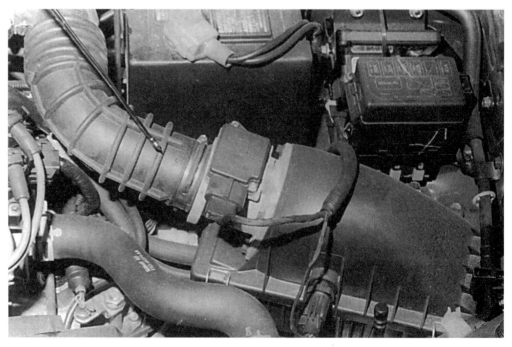

FIGURE 76
If the air-filter housing is not prominently positioned in the center of the engine, locate it by tracing the air duct from the carburetor, throttle body, or air intake.

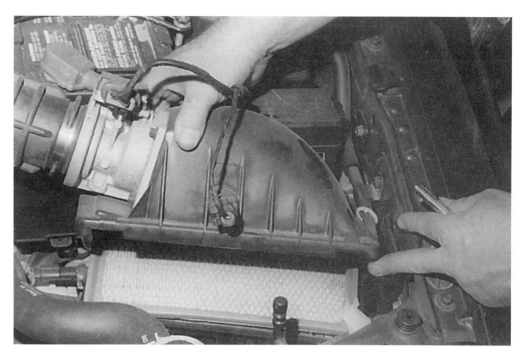

FIGURE 77
Loosen fasteners and open the housing.

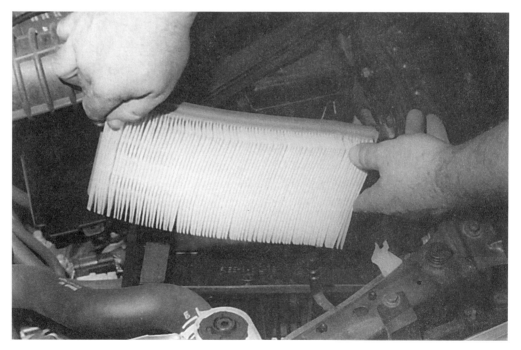

FIGURE 78
Remove and examine the air filter, replacing it if dirty.

housing may not be readily visible. If you have a problem locating it, trace the air duct back from the air intake until you come upon the filter housing. Open the housing by undoing the fastener securing the cover. Remove the old filter and install the new one.

PROBLEM: **No-start (engine doesn't crank or cranks too sluggishly to start)**

REPAIR: **Jump-start a discharged battery**

ENGINES: **All**

Jump-starting a discharged battery requires a set of jumper cables and an-other vehicle with a good battery. Before connecting jumper cables, re-move any rings, watch, or bracelets that you are wearing. Then, follow this procedure:

1. Maneuver the vehicle with the strong battery next to the one with the run-down battery, making sure that the two vehicles don't touch.
2. Turn off ignition switches, lights, and electrical accessories in both vehicles.
3. Shift the transmissions in both vehicles to Park or Neutral. Engage the parking brakes.
4. Open the hoods. If one or both of the batteries have vent caps, place a cloth over the tops of the caps. Batteries emit hydrogen through holes in vent caps. If exposed to a spark, hydrogen can ig-nite and cause the battery to explode.

CAUTION

Don't smoke.

---

5. Connect one of the jumper cables to the clamp of the cable at-tached to the positive side of the battery in the vehicle that doesn't start (Figure 79). Connect the other end of this jumper cable to the clamp of the cable attached to the positive side of the battery in the other vehicle.

IMPORTANT

Before going further, double-check connec-tions to make sure the jumper cable you have just connected is attached to the *positive* sides of both batteries. The positive side of a battery is marked + or POS.

FIGURE 79
To jump-start a dead battery, connect one of the jumper cables to the positive poles of the dead battery and the good (jumper) battery.

6. Connect the second jumper cable to the clamp of the cable attached to the negative side of the battery in the vehicle that does start. The negative side of a battery is marked – or NEG (Figure 80). Connect the other end of this jumper cable to a clean metal part of the engine in the vehicle that doesn't start (Figure 81). Place the clamp as far away from the weak battery as possible. An alternator bracket or an engine bolt that is large enough for the jaws of the clamp to bite into is a suitable spot.

CAUTION

Do not attach this jumper cable directly to the weak battery. If you do, a spark may occur, which may ignite any hydrogen that is being given off by the battery.

7. With everyone away from the engine compartments of the vehicles, start the engine of the vehicle with the strong battery. Then,

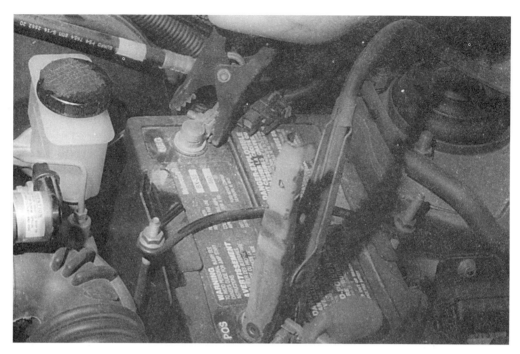

FIGURE 80
Connect the other jumper cable to the negative pole of the car possessing the good (jumper) battery.

FIGURE 81
Connect the other end of the jumper cable attached to the negative pole of the good (jumper) battery to a metal part of the car with the dead battery. The alternator bracket is generally suitable.

try starting the engine of the vehicle with the weak battery. If it doesn't start, turn off the ignition switches in both cars and check to make sure that both jumper cables are securely attached. Try again. If the engine of the vehicle with the weak battery still does not start, the problem is probably more serious than a run-down battery.

8. If the engine in the vehicle with the weak battery starts, let it run for several seconds. Then, with the engine still running, disconnect jumper cables in this order:

   ■ From the ground connection of the vehicle with the weak battery
   ■ From the negative side of the strong battery
   ■ From the positive side of the strong battery
   ■ From the positive side of the weak battery

PROBLEM: **No-start (engine doesn't crank or cranks too sluggishly to start)**

REPAIR: **Clean battery connections; charge or replace battery; test starter solenoid switch**

ENGINES: **All**

A battery has two jobs. One is to supply electricity to the starter motor so the starter can turn the engine crankshaft rapidly enough for the engine to start. The other is to provide current to operate electric accessories, such as the radio, heater, and lights, when the engine is not running.

When the engine is running, the battery is dormant. The current needed to operate electric accessories is provided by the alternating current (A/C) generator. The alternator, as the A/C generator is frequently called, also restores to the battery current that was expelled in helping to start the engine.

Inside the battery is sulfuric acid, which is often referred to as electrolyte or battery acid. Without this acid, the battery couldn't hold a charge. When your engine fails to crank or cranks too sluggishly to start, you can determine whether the battery is the cause of the problem by checking the strength of its sulfuric acid.

If your vehicle is equipped with a maintenance-free battery, look to see whether an indicator (sight glass) is present in the top of the battery (Figure 82). Peering into a sight glass lets you know the specific-gravity rating of the acid. Specific gravity is the weight of acid as compared to the weight of an equal volume of water.

Water has a specific-gravity rating of 1.000. Battery acid should have a specific-gravity rating of 1.230 to 1.300. If it doesn't, a battery may not be able to store enough current to start the engine.

As a battery gets older, the strength of its acid diminishes. When the specific-gravity rating falls to between 1.200 and 1.230, the battery may still have sufficient energy to help the starter motor crank the engine, except in cold weather when more power than the battery can supply is needed. But when the specific-gravity rating of electrolyte falls below 1.200, there won't be enough energy left in the battery—winter or summer—to start the engine.

What you see in the sight glass of a maintenance-free battery tells you one of three facts about the specific-gravity rating of the electrolyte (Figure 83):

1. If there is a green dot inside a black border, the specific gravity rating is between 1.230 and 1.300. The battery is probably not to

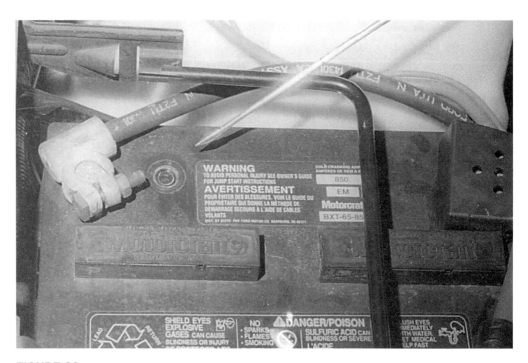

FIGURE 82
Most cars are equipped with maintenance-free batteries that have a sight glass on top to permit evaluation of battery acid strength.

blame for the engine failing to start. However, corrosion on battery cable terminals may be impeding the flow of current from the battery to the starter motor. Therefore, clean the cable terminals as described below to see whether this resolves the starting problem.

2. If only black appears in the sight glass, the specific-gravity rating of electrolyte is between 1.200 and 1.230. The battery could be

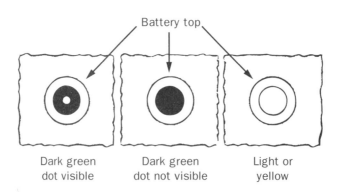

Battery top

Dark green dot visible   Dark green dot not visible   Light or yellow

FIGURE 83
One of the three indicators that you see in the sight glass tells you whether a battery is suitable (green dot), needs a charge (dark), or should be discarded (clear). (Courtesy of Chrysler Corporation)

causing your starting problem, especially in cold weather. Charge the battery.

There is another aspect to a "black" reading, especially if the battery is fairly new. Although the battery is probably okay, the alternator may not be providing it with a sufficient amount of current. Consequently, the battery may be forced to operate at a power level that cannot expel sufficient current to the starter motor. Have a technician who specializes in automotive electrical systems test alternator output to rule out the possibility, but first check belt tension (Figure 84).

3. If the sight glass of a maintenance-free battery is clear or light yellow, replace the battery. Do **not** charge it. When sulfuric acid reaches this point (a specific-gravity rating of less than 1.200), hydrogen trapped in the battery may ignite and cause the battery to explode if a charge is introduced.

Suppose your battery doesn't have a sight glass. Use a battery hydrometer, which you can buy from an auto parts store, to determine the specific-gravity rating of electrolyte (Figure 85). The hydrometer should have a built-in thermometer.

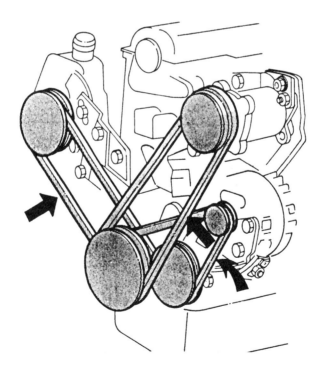

FIGURE 84
Engines may have as many as three belts to drive (from left) the power steering system, the air-conditioning system, and the alternator (charging system). (Courtesy of Chrysler Corporation)

FIGURE 85
A hydrometer is needed to test a nonmaintenance-free battery. (Courtesy of Chrysler Corporation)

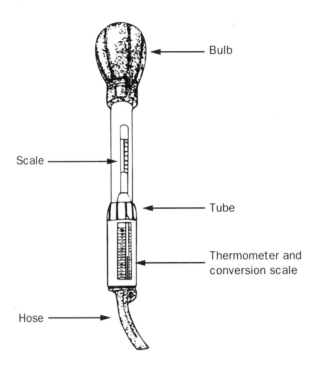

Bulb

Scale

Tube

Thermometer and conversion scale

Hose

Follow these steps to obtain the specific-gravity reading:

1. Unscrew the battery vent caps and check the level of the acid. If electrolyte in any cell is low, add distilled water, replace the vent caps, and drive the vehicle for a few hours before doing the test.
2. Insert the hydrometer hose into the first cell and squeeze the bulb to draw enough electrolyte into the hydrometer tube so that the scale floats in the liquid (Figure 86). Be careful not to draw too much acid into the tube; otherwise, the scale will jam against the top of the hydrometer and prevent an accurate reading.
3. Holding the scale at eye level, note where the numerals come to rest in relation to the top of the electrolyte. Jot down this reading. Then, check the temperature scale, which gives a correction factor relative to the temperature of the electrolyte. If the temperature of the electrolyte is 60°F, for example, the scale will tell you to subtract 0.008 from the hydrometer reading to get the true specific-gravity rating; if the temperature of the electrolyte is 100°F, you will have to add 0.008 to the reading.
4. Return the electrolyte to the cell from which it was drawn. Repeat the procedure to obtain the specific-gravity ratings of the electrolyte in the other cells.

FIGURE 86
Draw electrolyte into the hydrometer, record the reading, and return the electrolyte to the same battery cell from which it was drawn. Following this procedure, take readings from all the cells. (Courtesy of Chrysler Corporation)

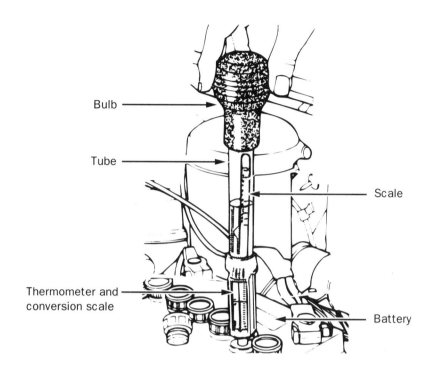

Bulb

Tube

Scale

Thermometer and conversion scale

Battery

CAUTION

Battery acid is dangerous. If it splashes onto your skin, immediately flush it off with water to prevent a burn. If acid should get into your eye, flush the eye with water and seek immediate medical attention. If some spills onto the vehicle, wash it off. Wear old clothes. Battery acid eats right through fabric. Do not smoke or bring anything near the vehicle that can cause a spark.

---

5. When you have all the readings, and have made the necessary compensation for temperature, compare readings with one another. If the readings from any two cells differ by more than 0.050 specific-gravity points, replace the battery. The low-reading cell is dead.

6. Add the readings together and divide by the number of cells (six) to get the overall specific-gravity rating of the electrolyte. As described above, a reading of 1.230 to 1.300 signifies a good battery. A reading of 1.200 to 1.230 indicates a battery that is borderline but

that may be strengthened by charging. A reading below 1.200 tells you that the battery should be replaced.

If your vehicle needs a new battery, consider purchasing a maintenance-free unit, which will eliminate frequent inspection to see that each cell is filled with electrolyte. The battery you buy should be rated at the cold cranking ampere (CCA) and hours reserve ratings recommended by the vehicle manufacturer. These ratings are inscribed on most original-equipment batteries (Figure 87). If your old battery is not original and you are uncertain as to what ratings your new battery should have, ask the service manager at a dealership that sells your make of vehicle.

When purchasing a new battery, make sure it has posts if your old battery has posts. If the cables of the old battery are attached to the side of the battery, your new battery should also have side-mountings.

The following procedure describes the proper way to replace a battery. Steps 1, 2, 7, 8, and 9 should be followed if the engine cranks too sluggishly to start and the battery passes the sight-glass or hydrometer test. These five steps explain how to service battery cable connections (terminals).

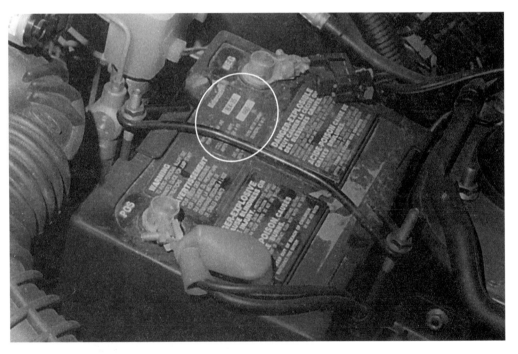

FIGURE 87
Labels on batteries offer important information, including a battery's cold cranking ampere (CCA) rating and hours reserve rating (circled).

C A U T I O N

Wear old clothes, work gloves, and eye protection.

1. Remove the ground cable (marked – or NEG) (Figure 88). If the cable is attached to a post, loosen the clamp and twist the terminal from side to side by hand. If this fails to remove the terminal from the post, use a battery cable puller to do the job (Figure 89). This tool is available from auto parts stores. Using any other tool may damage the battery.
2. Remove the positive cable (marked + or POS) in the same way.
3. Remove the battery hold-down clamp (Figure 90).
4. Use a battery carrier (strap) to lift the battery out of the vehicle.

NOTE Take the old battery to a service facility for proper disposal.

FIGURE 88
When working on a battery, always disconnect the ground (negative) cable first.

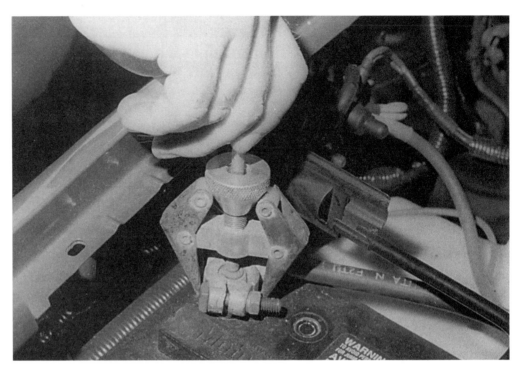

FIGURE 89
If you are unable to remove a cable from a battery post by hand, use a battery cable puller. Don't bang on the cable and post with a hammer. You could ruin the battery.

5. If the tray on which the battery sits is corroded, wash the tray with a mixture of baking soda and water. Baking soda eliminates corrosion and neutralizes the acid that causes corrosion. Flush the tray with clear water.

6. Using the battery strap, lift the new battery onto the tray and secure it with the hold-down clamp.

7. Use a wire brush to clean dirt and corrosion from cable terminals (Figure 91).

8. Connect the positive cable to the post or side-mounting marked + or POS. Tighten the fastener until it is snug. Then, connect the negative cable to the post or side-mounting marked – or NEG.

9. Spread a light coating of petroleum jelly across the cable terminals. This will help prevent corrosion.

Another possible culprit for an engine starting problem is a bad starter solenoid switch. If the switch is accessible (not part of the starter motor, that is), you can test it as illustrated in Figure 92.

FIGURE 90
The battery hold-down may be easy to release, as shown here. If the clamp secures the battery at the bottom, however, you may need a wrench with a long handle in order to reach it.

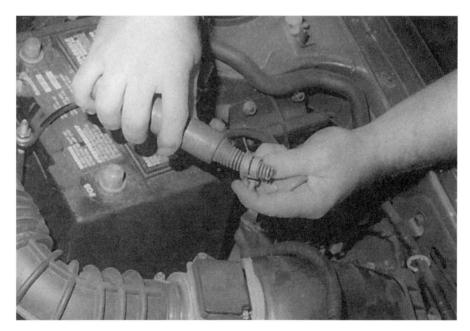

FIGURE 91
Corroded cable terminals could impede the flow of current to the battery and lead to an engine starting problem. Keep them clean.

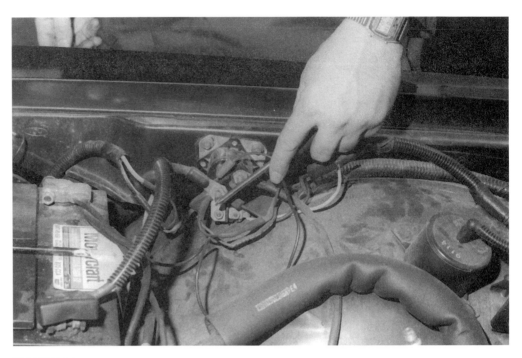

FIGURE 92
To test an accessible starter solenoid switch, which will be located near the battery (with a cable running between them), hold a screwdriver across the terminals of the switch. Have an assistant try to start the engine. If the engine starts, the switch will probably have to be replaced.

PROBLEM: **Oil loss**

REPAIR: **Alter oil-checking method**

ENGINES: **All**

Engine manufacturers contend that excessive oil consumption is a loss of two quarts of oil in 2,000 miles of driving. If your engine is using more than this, are you checking the oil level correctly? If you aren't, you may think your engine is using too much oil when in fact it isn't.

The correct way to check the quantity of oil in an engine is as follows:

1. With the engine warmed up, park the vehicle on level ground.
2. Turn off the engine.
3. Wait three minutes to allow oil in the upper reaches of the engine to flow back into the crankcase (oil pan).
4. Draw the oil-level indicator (dipstick) from the dipstick tube and wipe it off. Use a clean rag or paper towel to keep from getting dirt on the dipstick and then introducing it into the engine.
5. Reinsert the dipstick and push it all the way down into the tube.
6. Withdraw the dipstick and read the oil level.

Most dipsticks are marked FULL and ADD. The engine has a normal quantity of oil when the oil level is at the FULL mark or between the FULL and ADD marks.

If the level is on the ADD mark, the engine is one quart low. Never add oil unless the oil level is on or below the ADD mark. Doing so will cause an overfilled condition. Too much oil in an engine will cause foaming (air-filled bubbles), which will block oil and prevent it from reaching some engine parts. This can lead to abnormal wear.

PROBLEM: **Oil loss**

REPAIR: **Service PCV system**

ENGINE: **All**

In addition to causing rough idle or stalling (see page 114), a malfunctioning positive crankcase ventilation (PCV) system may be the reason why your engine is losing oil. If the PCV valve is not fully seated, oil will leak from around the valve. Press the valve firmly into the seat (Figure 93). Then, keep a watch on the oil level to determine whether this simple step has solved the problem.

If a PCV hose is kinked or clogged, causing an increase in pressure inside the crankcase, oil can be blown out of the crankcase and into the air-filter housing (Figures 94 and 95). Check to make sure that the PCV hose is straight (Figure 96).

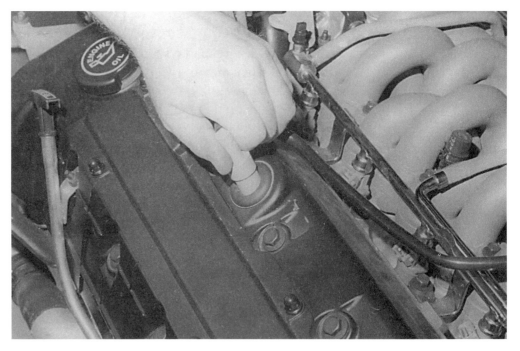

FIGURE 93
Press the PCV valve firmly into the engine to make certain that an unseated valve is not the reason for a loss of oil.

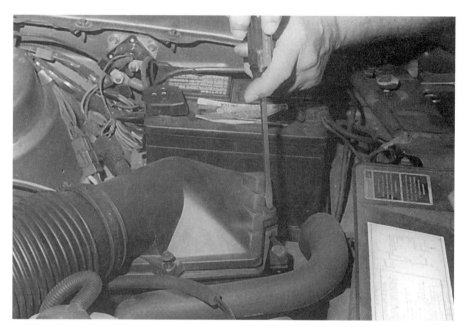

FIGURE 94
One way to determine whether a malfunctioning PCV system is causing a loss of oil is to open the air-filter housing.

FIGURE 95
Remove the air filter. If you find oil on the floor of the housing and/or on the filter, service the PCV system.

FIGURE 96
A PCV valve hose can cause excessive pressure that will force oil out of the crankcase. Make certain that the hose is straight.

PROBLEM: **Oil loss**

REPAIR: **Seal leaking oil pan**

ENGINES: **All**

Loss of oil may be the result of a leak around the oil-pan drain plug. A pool of oil found on the garage floor tips you off to this possibility.

The leak can occur when someone changing oil disregards the importance of the washer that was placed on the drain plug by the manufacturer.

This washer is made of a soft material, such as copper or aluminum, so that it will crush when the drain plug is tightened (Figure 97). The purpose is to prevent overtightening of the drain plug, which can damage the oil pan and cause a leak. To prevent this, the washer should be replaced whenever the drain plug is removed to change oil in the engine. Washers are available from dealerships that sell your make of vehicle and from auto parts stores.

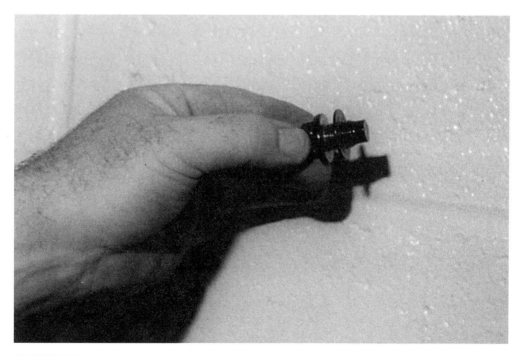

FIGURE 97
The washer of an oil-pan drain plug is designed to crush and prevent overtightening of the plug. It is recommended that this washer be replaced when the oil is changed.

If this advice comes too late and your oil pan currently is leaking, make the repair as follows:

1. Drive the vehicle at least 10 miles to heat the oil so that it will flow more readily from the engine.
2. Park the vehicle on level ground. Place an automatic transmission in Park or a manual transmission in gear. Engage the parking brake.

   > **NOTE** To make it easier for you to get under and out from under the vehicle, consider purchasing a creeper. This wheeled platform rolls so that you can maneuver easily as you lie upon it.

3. Wear a pair of heavy work gloves to prevent burns. Place a large basin under the oil pan and turn the drain plug with a wrench (Figure 98). When the plug is loose enough, unscrew it by hand.
4. Allow the oil ample time to drain fully. Drainage is complete when not one drop of oil falls from the drain hole in one minute.

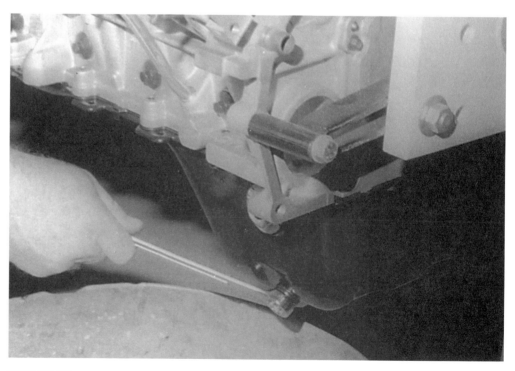

FIGURE 98
Changing the oil in an engine is one of the easiest tasks for a car owner to do.

5. Buy a specially made oversize drain plug from an auto parts dealer. The one you want is designed to rethread damaged threads in the oil pan, allowing the new plug to seat properly and seal the leak. Start the plug into the drain hole by hand, and then use a wrench to seat the plug. Stop turning as soon as the plug is secure.

6. Pour fresh oil into the engine through the oil filler tube in the engine compartment. Consult your owner's manual or a dealership that sells your make of vehicle to find out how much oil to add. Most engines hold five quarts of oil.

7. Start the engine and let it run for a few minutes. Then, turn it off and check to see whether oil leaks from around the plug. If there is a drip, tighten the drain plug a bit and recheck. If there is no leak, check the oil level using the dipstick and add as much oil as necessary to bring the level to or nearly to the FULL mark on the dipstick.

PROBLEM:	Overheating
REPAIR:	Replace radiator cap
ENGINES:	All

The radiator cap functions to increase the pressure that builds up in the engine cooling system and to seal the radiator in order to prevent loss of pressure or of the cooling agent, which is called coolant. By increasing the pressure above that which would otherwise build up in the cooling system, the radiator cap helps to raise the boiling point of the coolant by three degrees for each pound of pressure at which the cap is rated. Instead of boiling at 225°F, therefore, coolant in a radiator that uses a 15-pound cap won't boil unless it reaches 270°F. This provides an extra margin of safety, which can disappear if the cap loses its sealing ability—a possibility as the cap ages. As pressure escapes around a defective cap, the likelihood that the engine will begin to overheat increases.

An indication that a radiator cap has lost its effectiveness is when an engine overheats as it is operated under arduous conditions, such as in stop-and-go city driving on a hot day or when the vehicle is required to climb long, steep grades. Replacing the radiator cap—a simple step—may be the only repair that is needed.

CAUTION

Do this only when the engine is cold.

Every cap is rated at a particular pressure that varies from vehicle to vehicle. You must install a cap of the correct pressure for your cooling system. The pressure rating is usually embossed on the cap or is provided in the owner's manual. If you are unable to determine the correct rating, ask the salesperson in an auto supply store to look up the information in a parts manual.

PROBLEM: **Overheating**

REPAIR: **Apply a temporary repair for upper radiator hose**

ENGINES: **All**

Of all the hoses a cooling system possesses, the upper radiator hose is the one that is most likely to fail as you are driving (Figure 99). Coolant will gush from the cooling system through a hole in the hose, causing the engine to overheat quickly. You will be forced off the road to await a tow truck. You can avoid this by carrying the following emergency-repair equipment in your vehicle:

- Roll of two-inch duct tape
- Utility knife outfitted with a new blade
- Screwdriver
- Upper radiator hose repair kit (available from auto supply stores)
- Two plastic one-gallon containers filled with water
- Flashlight outfitted with fresh batteries to be used if a hose fails at night
- Heavy work gloves
- Eye protection

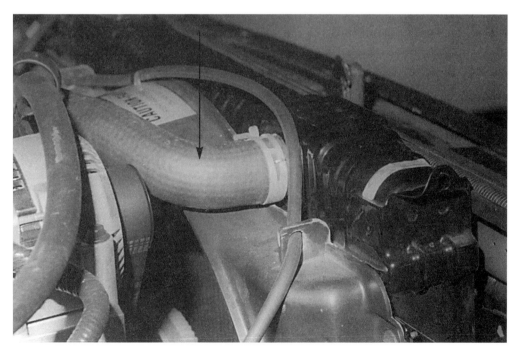

FIGURE 99
The upper radiator hose (arrow) is usually the hose that fails.

To temporarily repair an upper radiator hose, follow these steps:

CAUTION

The coolant will be hot enough to give you a first-degree burn. Unless you are sure you can do the repair safely, don't try it. Wait for the tow truck instead.

---

1. The moment you get a whiff of the strong, pungent odor that characterizes escaping coolant, pull off the road and turn off the engine.
2. Put on work gloves and eye protection, and open the hood.
3. Wrap several layers of duct tape around the tear in the hose to stem the loss (Figure 100). You will have no problem finding the split in the hose. You will see coolant coming out of it.

   NOTE This temporary measure may be enough to stop the loss of coolant until you can get home or to a repair shop and replace the hose; however, duct tape is not strong enough to hold back coolant under pressure for long.

4. If you are again forced off the road, wait about 30 minutes for the cooling system temperature to get low enough so you can work without being burned. Use the utility knife to splice the hose at the split. Cut away enough so you can slip the coupling in the repair kit onto the hose.

CAUTION

Don't forget to wear work gloves and eye protection.

---

5. Place the clamps in the repair kit on the coupling.
6. Attach the coupling to the two parts of the hose.
7. Position and tighten the clamps to lock the coupling and hose together.
8. Remove the radiator cap by pressing it down and turning until the cap hits the stop. Wait a few seconds for any pressure still in the cooling system to relieve itself before pressing down on the cap and turning it again to take it off.

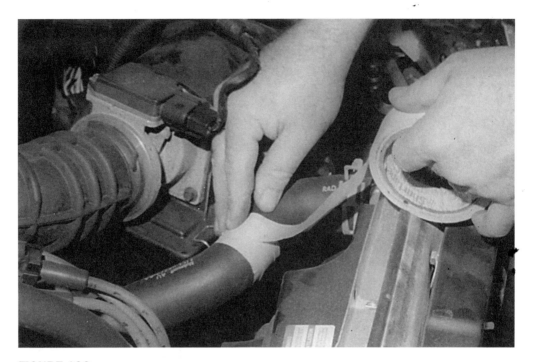

FIGURE 100
Several layers of duct tape wrapped around a hole in an upper radiator hose may be enough to stop a leak until you can get to a repair shop to have the hose replaced.

9. Pour water from the plastic containers into the radiator until it reaches the top of the radiator filler neck.

It is now safe to continue your trip. However, at the first opportunity replace the hose and fill the radiator with antifreeze (see pages 99 and 105).

PROBLEM: **Overheating at high speed only**

REPAIR: **Replace lower radiator hose**

ENGINES: **All**

A dashboard temperature light or temperature gauge that warns that an engine is overheating only when a vehicle is accelerated to a higher speed suggests that the lower radiator hose may be collapsing under pressure. The lower radiator hose possesses an internal support, usually in the form of a spring, that keeps the hose from drawing in when engine vacuum increases sharply, which happens during acceleration to a higher speed. If the hose collapses, the flow of coolant to the engine is temporarily cut off and the engine can overheat. When the driver lets up on the accelerator, the hose expands to a normal shape, and overheating usually dissipates.

If you encounter a problem such as this, you can find out whether the fault lies with the lower radiator hose by following these steps:

1. With the engine warmed up, park the vehicle. Place an automatic transmission in Park or a manual transmission in Neutral. Engage the parking brake. Leave the engine running.
2. Open the hood and locate the lower radiator hose (Figure 101).
3. As you watch the hose, ask an assistant in the vehicle to accelerate the engine sharply. If the hose draws in, losing its perfectly round shape, the support inside the hose has weakened. The hose should be replaced (see page 99).

FIGURE 101
The lower radiator hose becomes suspect if the engine overheats only when you are driving at highway speed. You can usually inspect the hose by looking down on it from above. Showing the hose in this car, however, required that it be photographed from below.

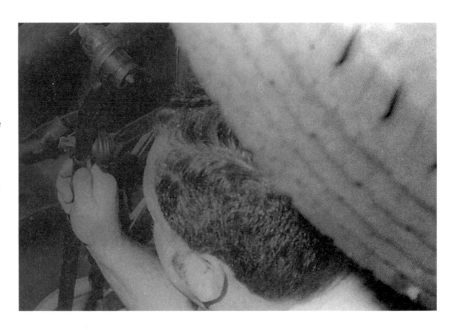

PROBLEM: **Overheating**

REPAIR: **Replace defective hoses; replace weakened coolant**

ENGINES: **All**

Every vehicle has at least five cooling-system hoses. Some have six (Figure 102). All must remain intact; otherwise, an engine will lose coolant and overheat.

Every vehicle has an upper radiator hose that transfers hot coolant from the engine to the radiator, and a lower radiator hose that transfers coolant from the radiator to the engine. Every vehicle also has two hoses that carry hot coolant to and away from the heater, and a coolant-recovery (overflow) hose.

The sixth hose on some engines is a bypass hose between the engine and the water pump (Figure 103). Its function is to direct coolant back into the engine when the engine is cold and the thermostat is closed. Engines without a bypass hose have an internal passage that directs coolant back into the engine when the thermostat is closed, blocking its path to the radiator.

FIGURE 102
This drawing illustrates hoses and other components of an automobile cooling system.

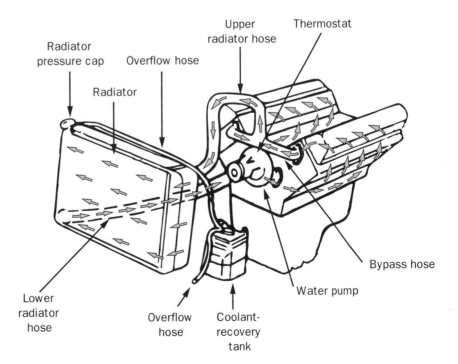

FIGURE 103
The coolant bypass hoses of some engines are longer than others—such as the one seen here, which extends from the thermostat housing to the engine. As long as the engine is cold and the thermostat is closed, coolant bypasses the radiator by circulating from the engine, through the hose, and back to the engine.

Some automotive authorities recommend that hoses be replaced every 60,000 miles. Others suggest that an inspection at 60,000 miles and every 10,000 miles thereafter is sufficient to spot a weak hose, which can then be replaced. They contend that it is unnecessary to replace hoses that are still usable.

If you decide to follow the latter suggestion, conduct the inspection with the engine cold. Examine both ends of a hose, around the clamps (Figure 104). Look for corrosive deposits, which indicate that the hose is starting to fail, allowing coolant to leak.

Squeeze the hose from one end to the other to determine whether there are cracks and also to feel the hose for firmness (Figure 105). A hose that feels "mushy" is a hose that is deteriorating internally.

Start the engine and let it warm up. Watch the hose. If a bulge forms, the hose should be replaced.

NOTE Test a lower radiator hose as described on page 98.

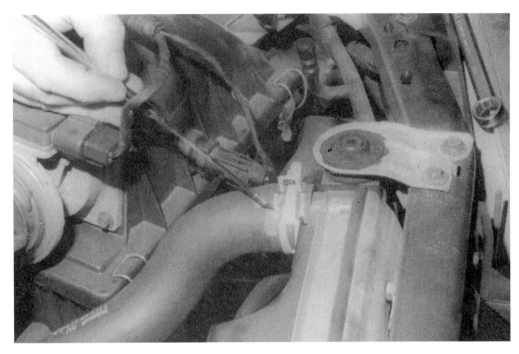

FIGURE 104
Corrosion around the clamp of a cooling system hose indicates a weakness at that spot.

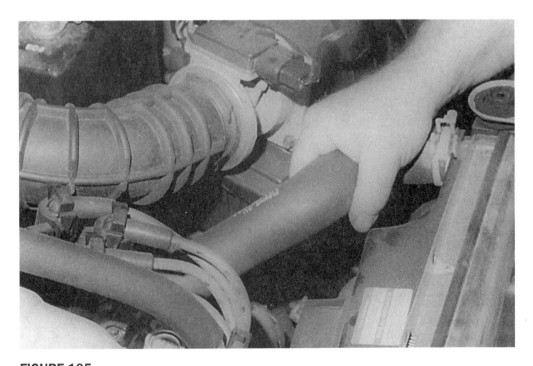

FIGURE 105
By squeezing a hose you will usually be able to determine whether there is deterioration.

Follow these steps to replace a suspicious-looking hose and to change coolant that has weakened.

Coolant should be replaced every two years or after every 30,000 miles of driving, whichever occurs first. Allowing weak coolant to remain in use will result in corrosion buildup in the cooling system. Corrosion can clog tubes in the radiator, causing the engine to overheat.

1. Let the engine get cold.
2. Place a large pan under the radiator drain valve, which is called the petcock.
3. Remove the radiator cap by pressing down and turning.
4. Open the petcock.

> **NOTE** If you own one of the few vehicles without a radiator petcock, you must remove the lower radiator hose to drain the coolant.

5. When coolant stops flowing, close the petcock.

IMPORTANT

Pour used coolant into gallon plastic jugs and contact the environmental agency in your municipality for proper disposal procedures.

---

6. Loosen clamps holding the ends of the defective hose and slide them from place (Figure 106). You will discard the used clamps, so there is no need to treat them gently (Figure 107). You can, in fact, cut them off.
7. Twist the end of the hose back and forth to release it from the fitting. If the hose sticks to the fitting and doesn't come off, cut lengthwise slits around the entire perimeter of the hose with a utility knife. Be careful not to cut into the fitting. Then, using a screwdriver, peel the pieces of hose off the fitting.
8. When the hose has been removed and discarded, use a wire brush to clean both fittings (Figure 108).
9. You are now ready to install the new hose, which should be the same length as the old hose. Place new clamps on the new hose (Figure 109). Then, soak the ends of the hose in hot water. This makes the hose pliable so that the ends can be pushed more easily onto the fittings.

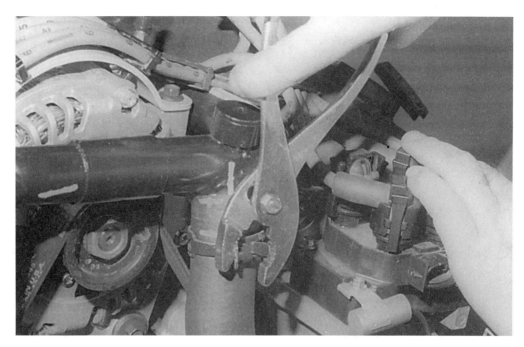

FIGURE 106
Release the hose clamp.

FIGURE 107
Discard the clamp. Take the hose off the fitting on the other end and discard the clamp on that end as well as the hose.

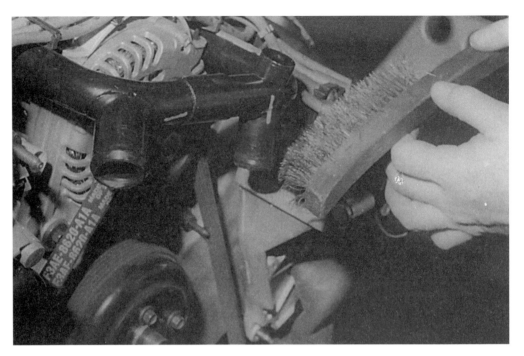

FIGURE 108
Before installing a new hose, clean fittings with a wire brush.

FIGURE 109
Slide new clamps onto the hose, press the hose on the fittings, and move clamps into position.

10. When the new hose is in place, slide the clamps into position, leaving a ⅛-inch gap between the ends of the hose and the edges of the clamps (Figure 110). Do not place the clamps right on the ends of the hose. Doing so may cause the hose to bulge at this point and release coolant.

11. Tighten clamps but don't ram them down.

12. Fill the radiator with a fresh coolant mixture consisting of half ethylene glycol and half water. A 50:50 ratio protects engines to a temperature of about −20°F. If a lower temperature than this is anticipated for your part of the country, check the owner's manual for the proper ratio or ask at an auto parts store. Do not exceed a ratio of 68 percent ethylene glycol to 32 percent water, which will protect an engine to about −90°F. Once this ratio is exceeded, the protection factor reverses itself. In fact, using full-strength ethylene glycol in an engine provides protection only to about −8°F.

13. Put on and tighten the radiator cap.

14. Fill the coolant-recovery tank with coolant to the COLD mark.

15. Start the engine and let it run for two minutes. Turn it off and check around the ends of the hose. If coolant is leaking, tighten the clamp a bit more. Repeat this procedure until the leak stops.

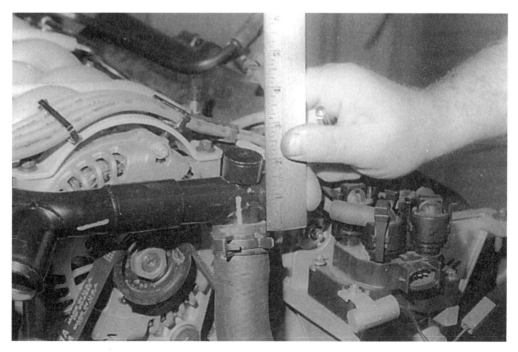

FIGURE 110
Clamps should be placed about ⅛ inch from the ends of the hose.

PROBLEM: **Overheating**

REPAIR: **Apply a temporary repair for radiator**

ENGINES: **All**

Suppose you are driving along when the radiator starts to leak. Even if you have enough time to get to a repair shop before the engine overheats, there is no guarantee that you can have a new radiator installed. Maybe it's Sunday. Maybe it's late at night. What do you do? Try this:

1. When you get that first whiff indicating that the engine is losing coolant, or you see that first wisp of white vapor escaping from under the hood, pull off the road and turn off the engine.
2. Open the hood and examine the radiator. If the leak is coming from one of the radiator tanks, you won't be able to make this repair. If coolant is leaking from the core of the radiator, proceed with the repair if the proper tools and equipment are available (Figure 111).
3. Use pliers to tear away the radiator fins from around where you see coolant leaking until you come upon the one internal tube that is damaged (Figure 112). That tube will be obvious, because coolant will be ebbing out of it.

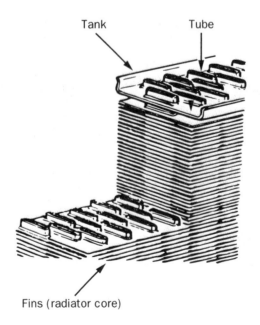

Tank   Tube

Fins (radiator core)

FIGURE 111
A radiator consists of top and bottom tanks, a series of tubes that extend between the two tanks, and fins that cover the tubes.

FIGURE 112
By stripping away the fins to uncover a leaking tube, you can crimp the tube closed and continue driving.

CAUTION

Wear heavy work gloves to protect your hands. Touching a hot radiator or being touched by hot coolant can cause a severe burn.

---

4. When you identify the leaking tube, use your pliers to crimp it closed. This will stop the leak.

5. Wait about 30 minutes for the radiator to cool before removing the cap and refilling the radiator with water, which, if you're prepared, you will be carrying in two one-gallon plastic containers.

> **NOTE** Have the radiator replaced as soon as possible.

PROBLEM:	Overheating
REPAIR:	Replace cooling-fan switch
ENGINES:	All with electric cooling fans

Vehicles that are equipped with electric cooling fans have switches that sense the temperature of the coolant and turn the fan on when the temperature reaches a preset level. If this does not happen, coolant will boil and the engine will overheat.

Testing this switch to find out whether it is the reason for overheating is not a difficult task. However, you will need an ohmmeter.

Here is what to do:

1. To find out whether the cause of overheating is failure of the fan to turn on, start the engine (which must be cold), open the hood, and watch the fan as the engine warms up.

CAUTION

Keep away from the fan, which will start without warning if the switch is not defective.

2. Let the engine run for several minutes, but ask a helper sitting in the vehicle to turn off the engine if the temperature warning light on the dash should glow or if the needle of the temperature gauge approaches the HOT mark.

   Does the fan begin to rotate during this period? If it does, the cause of overheating does not lie with the cooling-fan switch.
3. If the fan does not begin to spin, turn off the engine and wait for the engine to again get cold before testing the cooling-fan switch.
4. After the waiting period, trace the wire from the fan motor to the electrical connector (Figure 113).
5. Pull apart the connector, disconnecting the fan from the electrical system.
6. Trace the wire from the connector to where it attaches to the cooling-fan switch, which is screwed either into the tank of the radiator or into the engine (Figure 114).
7. Pull the wire off the cooling-fan switch.
8. Use a wrench to unscrew the switch from the radiator tank or from the engine.

FIGURE 113
To find the cooling-fan switch, trace the wire from the fan motor. Keep your hands away from the blades. (Courtesy of Chrysler Corporation)

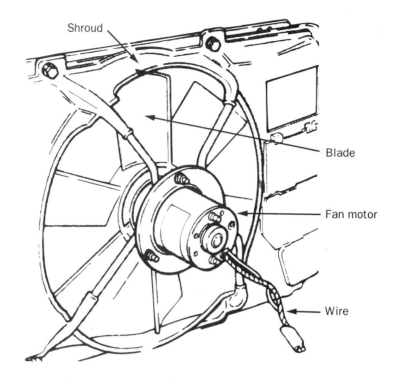

Shroud

Blade

Fan motor

Wire

NOTE You will have to drain coolant before removing the switch (see page 99).

9. To verify that the switch has failed, place the switch in a pan of water, but do not immerse its terminal end. Some switches have one terminal; others have two. If the switch has one terminal, also keep the threads around the terminal out of the water. Place a kitchen thermometer in the pan with the switch and set the pan on a kitchen stove burner.

10. Test the switch using an ohmmeter. If the switch has one terminal, touch one of the ohmmeter probes to the terminal and touch the other probe to the threads. If the switch has two terminals, touch each ohmmeter probe to a terminal. The ohmmeter should display an infinity reading.

11. Turn on the stove burner. When the thermometer indicates that the water has reached at least 220°F, repeat the ohmmeter test. The ohmmeter needle should swing to 0 or nearly to 0. If it doesn't, the switch is defective.

If the switch has failed, buy a replacement that is specified for the cooling system of your vehicle from a dealership parts depart-

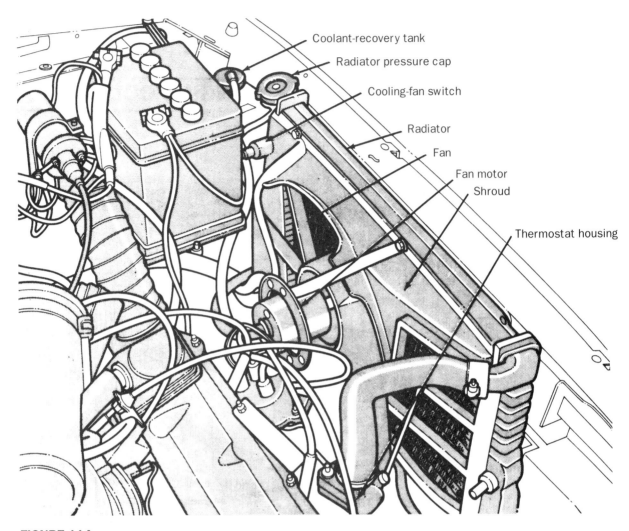

FIGURE 114
This illustration identifies parts of a typical automotive cooling system. Note the position of the cooling-fan switch. (Courtesy of Chrysler Corporation)

ment or from an auto parts store. Coat the threads of the new switch with pipe thread sealer or wrap them with teflon plumbing tape. This will prevent a leak. Screw the switch in place by hand until it is fingertight. Then, use a wrench to tighten the switch.

Fill the cooling system with coolant. Start the engine, let it run a while, and turn it off. Check around the switch to make certain that there is no leak.

PROBLEM: **Overheating**

REPAIR: **Seal leaking head gasket**

ENGINES: **All**

Replacing a cylinder head gasket that is allowing coolant to leak from the engine costs several hundred dollars. Before turning the vehicle over to a professional mechanic, try this simple procedure, which may stop the leak for an indefinite period:

1. With the engine cold, remove the radiator cap.
2. Replenish coolant, if necessary.
3. Drop pellets of sealing compound into the radiator according to the directions on the package.

> **NOTE** Pellets sold for this purpose at General Motors dealerships have proved particularly effective.

4. Put on the radiator cap and drive the vehicle several hundred miles before judging whether the cylinder head gasket has been sealed.

PROBLEM: **Rough idle**

REPAIR: **Tighten loose carburetor or throttle body bolts; replace defective carburetor or throttle body gasket**

ENGINES: **Carburetor, TBI**

If the bolts that hold the carburetor or throttle body to the intake manifold loosen, too much air will enter the manifold and dilute the fuel mixture. A lean fuel mixture causes an engine to idle rough. Remove the air-filter housing and tighten each carburetor and throttle body bolt (Figure 115).

It is also possible for the gasket between the carburetor or throttle body and the intake manifold to deteriorate over a period of time, leaving a gap that allows an infusion of air. To determine whether this has happened, do the following:

1. Use a carburetor solvent spray or mix equal amounts of SAE 30 motor oil and kerosene, pouring the mixture into a squeeze-type oilcan outfitted with a long nozzle.

Tighten bolts

FIGURE 115
Tightening throttle body or carburetor bolts may be all that's necessary to prevent excess air from entering the fuel and thus causing the engine to idle rough.

2. Start the engine, which will idle roughly.

3. Spread the mixture around the joint formed where the carburetor or throttle body joins the intake manifold (Figure 116).

If the idle becomes smooth, even momentarily, it confirms the existence of a deteriorated gasket. Tell a mechanic of your findings.

CAUTION

In doing this test, stay clear of pulleys, drive belts, and the cooling fan.

FIGURE 116
If spraying the joint between a throttle body or carburetor and the intake manifold causes engine idle to become smooth, the gasket between the two should be replaced.

PROBLEMS: **Rough idle, stalling**

REPAIR: **Replace PCV valve, PCV hose, PCV dirt trap**

ENGINES: **All**

Most engines manufactured since the 1960s have a positive crankcase ventilation (PCV) system, which prevents hydrocarbon vapors in the crankcase from escaping into and polluting the atmosphere. The central component of this system is the PCV valve, which is a main concern when an engine begins to idle roughly and/or stall (Figure 117).

Two other parts of the system can also cause trouble. One is the hose attached to the PCV valve (Figures 118 and 119). The other is a dirt trap that screens the air that is ingested by the crankcase to assist in the burning of hydrocarbon vapors (Figure 120).

A malfunctioning PCV system may be signaled by an oily residue on the air filter or by oil in the air-filter housing—a consequence of a faulty PCV component creating a pressure buildup in the crankcase. Trapped pressure forces oil out of the crankcase and into the air-filter housing, where it coats the air filter and/or causes oil to puddle on the floor of the housing.

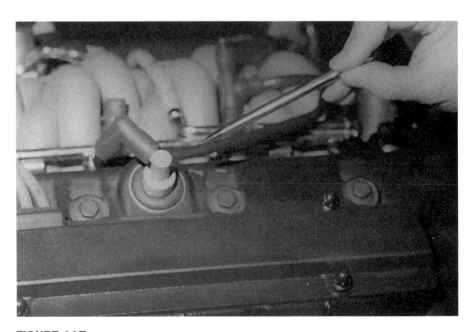

FIGURE 117
The PCV system, which has the PCV valve as its main component, is the oldest of automotive emissions-control systems. It is also one of the most neglected insofar as servicing is concerned.

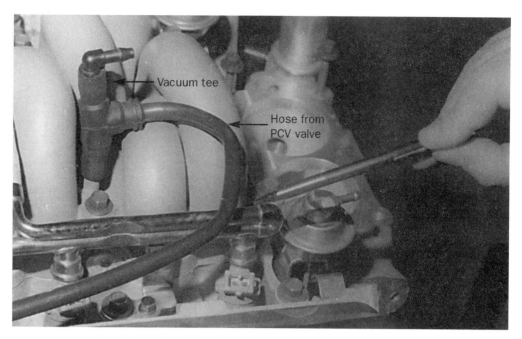

FIGURE 118

The PCV systems of some engines, such as this one with a multiport fuel-injection system, are more elaborate than others. The hose here extends from the PCV valve shown in Figure 117 to a vacuum fitting (or tee). All parts should be inspected when a performance problem arises that might be caused by a malfunctioning PCV system.

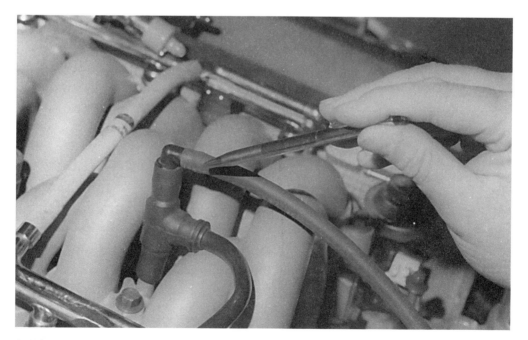

FIGURE 119

The vacuum tee has a second hose connected to it that is also part of the PCV system and that should be included in the inspection procedure.

FIGURE 120
Most (not all) engines with carburetor or TBI fuel systems are equipped with a dirt trap (filter) to screen air that is used by the PCV system. This drawing shows the arrangement used by most General Motors cars. The dirt trap is in the air-filter housing. It can be removed by slipping off a retaining clip. (Courtesy of General Motors)

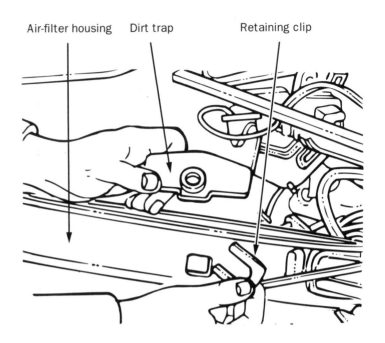

Air-filter housing   Dirt trap   Retaining clip

By itself, the presence of oil in the air-filter housing does not necessarily indicate a faulty PCV system. Oil can be deposited on the filter or in the housing if valve guide seals inside the engine are worn. Furthermore, oil isn't always present when a PCV valve, PCV hose, or PCV dirt trap fails. A closer examination of the system, therefore, is necessary. Here is how to make this inspection:

1. With the engine turned off, pull the PCV valve from its seat, which could be in a rocker arm cover, intake manifold, or oil-filler cap (Figure 121). If you can't locate the valve, ask a mechanic or a service manager at a dealership that sells your make of vehicle to point it out.

2. Have an assistant start the engine.

CAUTION

Keep your hands away from belts, pulleys, and the cooling fan.

3. Hold your thumb tightly over the end of the valve (Figure 122). If you feel no suction, the valve is clogged. Turn off the engine and replace the valve.

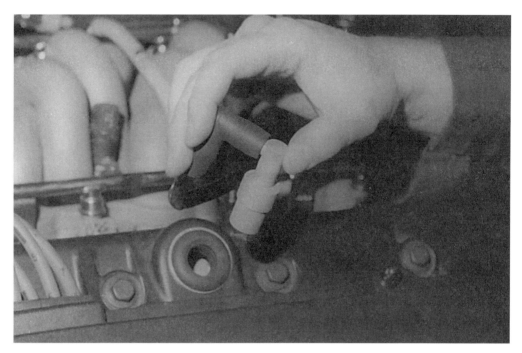

FIGURE 121
To test the PCV valve, pull it out of its seat.

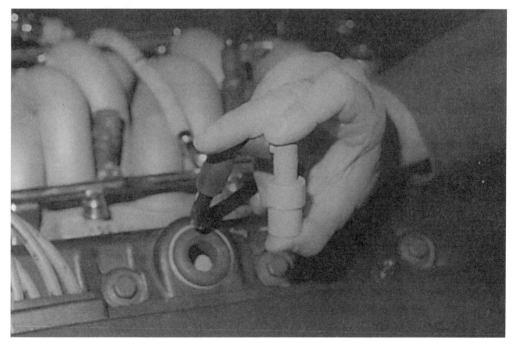

FIGURE 122
With the engine running at idle, hold your thumb firmly over the valve opening.

4. Even if you do feel suction, the valve still may not be performing properly, because the mechanism inside the valve may be sticking. To check this possibility, pull the valve and hose apart (Figure 123). Then, shake the valve. If you hear a rattle, the valve is okay. If not, take the valve to the parts department of a dealer who sells your make of vehicle or to an auto parts store and buy a new one.

5. The next step is to examine the PCV hose for cracks and to make sure it has no kinks that can trap vapors and prevent free circulation (Figure 124). Replace a damaged hose.

6. Replace the PCV dirt trap, which is inside the air-filter housing. Look for it around the rim of the housing. Again, if you can't find it, ask a technician to point it out.

With some engines, the dirt trap is inserted in a hole in the rim of the air-filter housing. Simply pull it out of the hole and shove in a new one. Other engines require you to remove a clip on the outside of the air-filter housing to release a hose. You then push the dirt trap out of the filter housing.

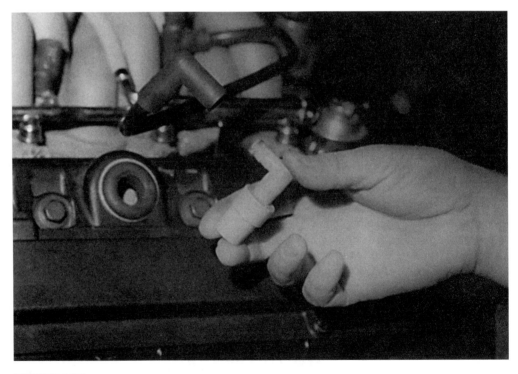

FIGURE 123
Disconnect the valve from the hose and shake the valve. A rattling sound means that the valve is still working.

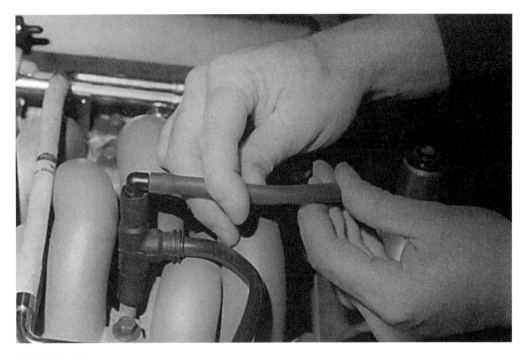

FIGURE 124
Inspect all hoses that are part of the PCV system. Replace a hose if it shows any sign of cracking. Hoses must run straight or in a smooth arc.

PROBLEMS: **Rough idle, stalling**

REPAIR: **Service EVAP system**

ENGINES: **All**

EVAP, an abbreviation for fuel evaporation control system, prevents gasoline vapors from escaping into and polluting the atmosphere. When an EVAP system sustains damage, an engine can idle roughly and/or stall, and there will probably be a strong odor of gasoline.

The heart of the EVAP system is a charcoal canister that absorbs vapors, which enter the canister from the fuel system through hoses (Figure 125). As the engine runs, vapors are drawn into the cylinders and are burned. The performance problem and odor of gasoline arise if the canister cracks, if one of the hoses is damaged, or if a filter inside the canister clogs.

NOTE Not all EVAP charcoal canisters have filters.

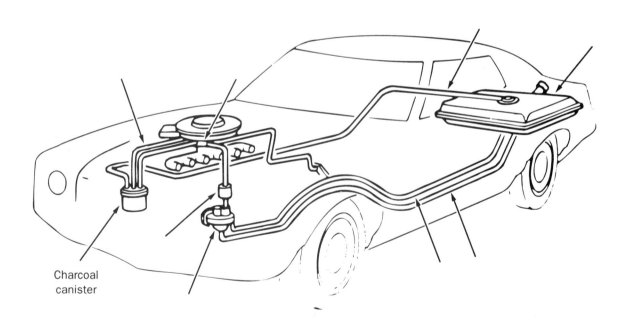

Charcoal
canister

FIGURE 125
An engine equipped with a carburetor, as here, or a fuel-injection system has a fuel evaporation control system. Vapors from all fuel system components (arrows) flow into a charcoal canister.

Here is how to repair a vehicle's EVAP system:

1. Find the charcoal canister.
2. Using self-adhering labels, identify each hose in terms of the canister fitting to which it is connected (Figure 126). Later, each must be reattached to the correct fitting.
3. Loosen clamps and pull off hoses.
4. Loosen the bracket holding the canister, and remove the canister from the vehicle.
5. Inspect the canister for damage. Pay particular attention to the area around hose fittings. If you find a crack, take the component to the parts department of a dealer who sells your make of vehicle and buy a new one.
6. Turn the canister over to find out whether it has a filter, which should be replaced before you reinstall an undamaged canister.

> **NOTE** If this fails to solve the performance problem and to eliminate the gasoline odor, replace the canister. A canister without a filter has an estimated life expectancy of 50,000 miles.

7. Inspect hoses and replace any that are cracked.
8. Install the canister and connect hoses to their proper fittings, making sure that clamps are secure.

FIGURE 126
After disconnecting hoses and removing the charcoal vapor canister from a vehicle, turn the canister upside down to determine whether it's equipped with a filter. If it is, replace the filter. (Courtesy of Chrysler Corporation)

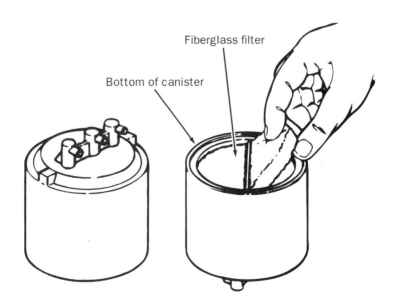

Fiberglass filter

Bottom of canister

PROBLEM:	**Stalling in wet weather only**
REPAIR:	**Service ignition or fuel system**
ENGINES:	**All**

The repairs described in this section apply only if the engine of your vehicle stalls in wet weather, which includes periods of high atmospheric humidity even when rain or snow is not falling. If wet-weather stalling occurs suddenly, without warning, one set of factors is involved. If wet-weather stalling occurs over a period of seconds during which the vehicle bucks, another set of factors is involved. The repair(s) that should be attempted depends on how stalling takes place, as follows:

SUDDEN STALLING IN WET WEATHER. The engine starts normally and runs perfectly, but after several miles of driving it suddenly stalls without warning. Attempts at restarting within the first 30 to 60 minutes after the stall takes place usually fail. Ambient temperature is not a factor. The only common denominator is wet weather.

If you have been experiencing this type of problem, fill a spray bottle with water. Start the engine and let it idle as you spray water over the distributor cap. Make sure you spray the entire surface of the cap with an ample amount of water. If the engine stalls, the trouble lies inside the distributor.

Turn off the ignition switch and remove the cap. Examine the inside for a trace of carbon, which if found means that the cap is cracked (Figure 127). Replace the cap with a new one.

Next, turn your attention to the distributor rotor (Figure 128). Examine the rotor closely by removing it from the distributor shaft. Look for corrosion on the metal terminal and for cracks in the body of the rotor. Replace a damaged rotor.

The pickup coil is another critical part inside the distributor that has to be considered when sudden wet-weather stalling becomes a problem. Testing and replacing this part are tasks best left to a mechanic.

If the engine doesn't stall after the distributor cap has been sprayed with water, spray every electrical connector you can find. Electrical connectors are two-part assemblies that are held together with clips (Figure 129). Again, use a lot of water.

If the engine now stalls, here is what to do:

1. Turn off the ignition switch.
2. Unclip and pull apart the connector (Figure 130).

FIGURE 127
Replace a cracked distributor cap.

FIGURE 128
Remove the rotor from the distributor shaft and examine it closely. Replace the rotor if cracked or if the metal pickup terminal is corroded or burned.

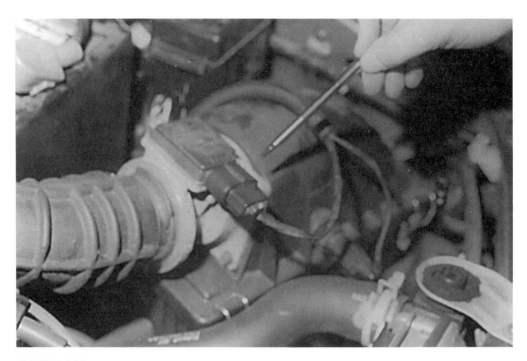

FIGURE 129
Use the test described in the text to check all electrical connectors, such as this one servicing the mass air-flow sensor, if your engine stalls only in wet weather.

3. Examine both halves of the connector for cracks. Have a mechanic replace a cracked connector.
4. Inspect the pins in the male half of the connector to see whether any are bent. Straighten bent pins with needle-nose pliers (Figure 131).
5. Use a thin wire brush to clean the insides of both halves of the connector.
6. Spread a thin coating of dielectric grease inside the male half of the connector (Figure 132). Dielectric grease, which is a special lubricant that resists water without impeding the flow of current, can be purchased from an auto supply store or from a store that sells electronic equipment.
7. Press the two halves of the connector firmly together and secure them with the clips.

DELAYED STALLING IN WET WEATHER. This type of wet-weather stalling occurs when the ambient temperature is between 35 and 50°F. The engine starts and runs perfectly, but after a few miles of driving it begins to stutter as if running out of gas. After several seconds of this behavior, it stalls but can usually be restarted after sitting idle for about 15 minutes.

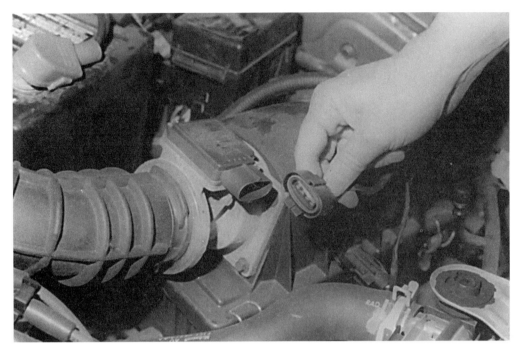

FIGURE 130
To repair electrical connectors that are the cause of wet-weather stalling, pull them apart.

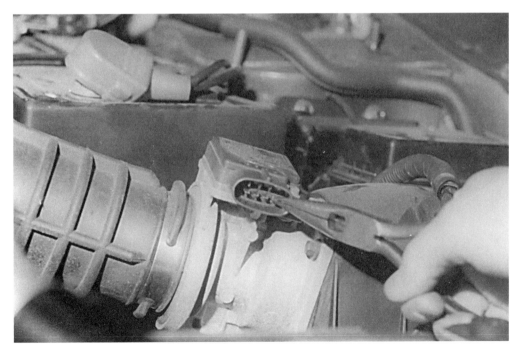

FIGURE 131
Straighten bent pins in the male half of the connector.

FIGURE 132
Apply a thin coat of dielectric grease to the connector.

This problem occurs when condensation forms inside the carburetor or throttle body, fuel line, or fuel tank and turns to ice, reducing the flow of fuel to the engine. To prevent the condition, keep the fuel tank as full as possible. Pouring cans of a fuel-system antifreeze into the fuel tank during the time of year when the fuel system is likely to ice up is another preventive method. Be sure that the liquid is compatible with your engine's type of fuel system.

PART II
Nonengine Problems

The engine repairs described in Part I generally crop up more frequently than the repairs for the problems described in this section of the book. Be that as it may, the cost of having a nonengine problem repaired by a professional mechanic can often equal or even exceed the amount of money you would have to lay out to have that mechanic repair an engine performance problem.

This part of the book outlines easy-to-do instructions for making repairs to vehicle components or systems that do not affect engine performance. Most of the repairs can be done in a few minutes; some take an hour or two. None requires special tools or instruments.

The repairs described here have been chosen on the basis of an evaluation of letters that I have received from vehicle owners since 1962, first as author of "Car Clinic" in *Popular Mechanics* for 26 years and then as author of "Handyman Garage Service" in *The Family Handyman,* a *Reader's Digest* service publication. Readers of the two magazines have most often solicited repair advice about the following nonengine problems:

(continued)

COMPONENT: **Automatic transmission**

PROBLEMS: **Failure to shift normally; fluid leak from transmission pan**

By following the procedure described below, you may be able to repair an automatic transmission that is slipping. "Slipping" is the term applied to a transmission that doesn't shift gears at the proper time. The condition is identified by a lag in upshifting as engine speed increases.

It is important to note that the repair is actually the severe service maintenance procedure suggested by vehicle manufacturers to prevent slippage from occurring in the first place. Manufacturers claim that performing this service every 25,000 miles, if you operate your vehicle under severe driving conditions, will prevent failure of an automatic transmission. Severe driving conditions are the following:

- Operating a vehicle primarily in stop-and-go city traffic most of the time.
- Operating a vehicle more than half the time in stop-and-go city traffic when the ambient temperature is 90°F or higher.
- Using a vehicle to tow a trailer.
- Driving a vehicle primarily in a dusty environment.
- Driving a vehicle primarily over hills or mountains.

These severe driving conditions cause fluid in an automatic transmission to overheat and become contaminated. The fluid then loses its ability to protect delicate parts of a transmission, which will sustain damage.

Periodically draining and examining automatic transmission fluid in a vehicle used under one or more severe conditions will allow you to detect the onset of trouble. If failure has already occurred and a transmission is slipping, replacing the fluid could also resolve the problem.

Whether you are attempting to repair an automatic transmission that is slipping or have decided to implement a maintenance program to ward off trouble, the following describes what to do. Suppose, however, the problem you're having is not a slipping transmission, but a fluid leak from around the transmission pan. The same instructions can be followed to repair the leak.

1. Drive the vehicle at least 10 miles to heat the transmission fluid.
2. Park the vehicle on a level surface, shut off the engine, place the transmission shift selector in Park, and engage the parking brake.

CAUTION

If you do not have the necessary equipment mentioned below to support the vehicle while you are under it, do _not_ do this repair.

3. Jack up the front of the vehicle.
4. Place a support stand under each front control arm and lower the vehicle onto the stands.
5. Ram chocks against both sides of each rear tire to prevent the vehicle from rolling back.
6. Place a large pan under the transmission pan.
7. Remove the bolts by starting at a corner, so that the corner drops lower than the rest of the transmission pan, and allow fluid to flow into the other pan (Figure 133).
8. Take out the remaining bolts and remove the transmission pan.

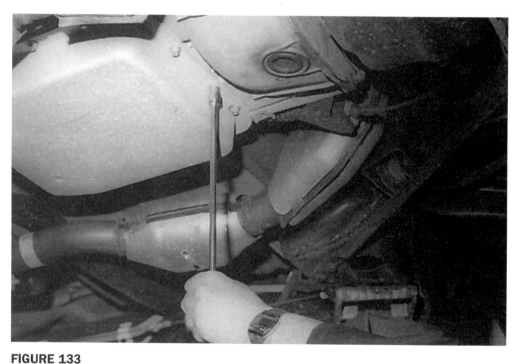

FIGURE 133
Drain an automatic transmission by loosening bolts and removing the transmission pan.

CAUTION

Wear eye protection and gloves when draining automatic transmission fluid.

9. Before discarding the fluid that remains in the bottom of the transmission pan, inspect it for particles, color, and odor.

   Slosh the fluid back and forth. The presence of fine black and/or brass residue is normal. However, if larger pieces are visible, pour the fluid containing the particles into a clean jar and take it to a transmission specialist. The specialist will be able to determine what should be done to prevent damage from progressing to an advanced stage.

   Fluid should be red. If it looks muddy and/or smells like varnish, filling the transmission with fresh fluid may straighten out a slipping condition.

   Incidentally, if fluid is white, the transmission oil cooler has a leak that is allowing coolant to mix with transmission fluid. Take the vehicle to an automotive radiator shop to have the cooler replaced.

IMPORTANT

Pour the transmission fluid into glass bottles. Cap the bottles and label them "CAUTION: TOXIC AUTOMATIC TRANSMISSION FLUID." Then, check with environmental officials in your municipality for proper disposal procedures.

10. Continue the repair by peeling or scraping off the gasket from the rim of the transmission pan and from the rim of the transmission body. All of this material must be removed or it will prevent the pan from seating securely to the transmission. This will cause a fluid leak.

11. Using a nonflammable solvent, which is available from an auto supply store, wash the pan.

12. Locate the transmission fluid filter inside the transmission. It is out in the open and easily reached (Figure 134). Remove the screw(s) that hold the filter in place and take the filter out of the transmission.

FIGURE 134
When you remove the transmission pan, the transmission fluid filter is exposed. Service or replace it. (Courtesy of Chrysler Corporation)

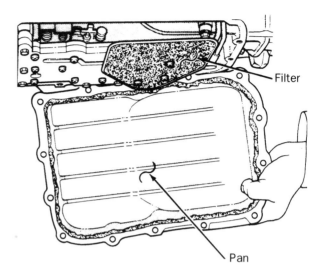

Filter

Pan

If the filter is made of paper or felt, replace it. If it is made of metal, wash it in nonflammable solvent and put it back into the transmission.

13. Place a new gasket on the rim of the transmission pan so that the holes in the gasket align with the holes in the rim of the pan. Make sure the gasket lies straight as you place the pan against the body of the transmission, and insert the bolts.

14. When all bolts are in place, tighten a bolt using a wrench. Then, tighten the bolt that lies diagonally across from the one you just tightened. Follow this pattern to tighten all the bolts.

15. Remove the automatic transmission fluid dipstick (Figure 135). Wipe it with a clean cloth and place it where it won't become dirty.

16. Insert a clean funnel into the dipstick tube and pour in one quart of the type of automatic transmission fluid recommended by the vehicle manufacturer (Figure 136). This information can be found in your owner's manual. Use only this fluid, as any other type can cause transmission damage.

17. Reinsert the dipstick and pull it out again to check the fluid level. Continue filling the transmission in this manner until the fluid level hits the FULL mark on the dipstick.

18. With the dipstick seated in the dipstick tube, start the engine and let it warm up for five minutes. Then, move the transmission shift lever through all gears and back again toward Park, pausing momentarily between each shift. Keep your foot planted firmly on the brake pedal to prevent the vehicle from moving.

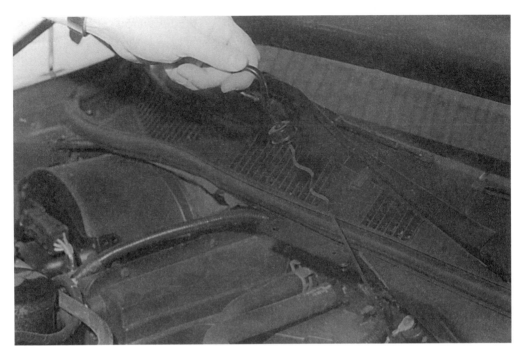

FIGURE 135
The automatic transmission dipstick is found in the rear of the engine compartment.

FIGURE 136
Make sure that the fluid you use in an automatic transmission is the type recommended by the vehicle manufacturer.

19. With the shift lever again in Park, turn off the engine and withdraw the fluid dipstick to check the fluid level. If it has dropped below FULL, add enough fluid to bring it back to that mark or a little below. Be careful not to exceed the FULL mark (Figure 137). Too much fluid in an automatic transmission will cause the transmission to slip.

20. Over the next few days, check the fluid level often and keep an eye on the ground where you park the vehicle. If the level drops and/or you notice fluid on the ground under where the transmission was positioned, the pan is leaking. Tighten the bolts a bit more. If the leak persists, you may have damaged the gasket and should install a new one.

Draining the transmission will not get rid of all the old fluid. Some will be trapped in the torque converter. If the torque converter in your car doesn't have a drain plug, you will have to repeat the drainage procedure twice more after driving the vehicle in increments of 5,000 miles (Figure 138). There is, however, an easier solution. Have a $\frac{1}{2}$-inch threaded drain plug installed in the transmission pan at a transmission shop.

With a drain plug in the transmission pan, drive the vehicle for 5,000 miles so that the fresh fluid you put in the transmission mixes with the old fluid trapped in the torque converter. You can then drain fluid by simply removing the drain plug.

FIGURE 137
Do not overfill an automatic transmission. The fluid level should not be above the FULL mark. (Courtesy of Chrysler Corporation)

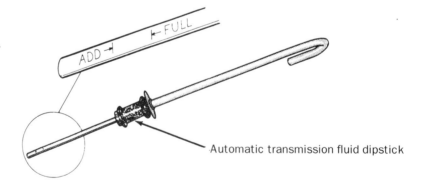

Automatic transmission fluid dipstick

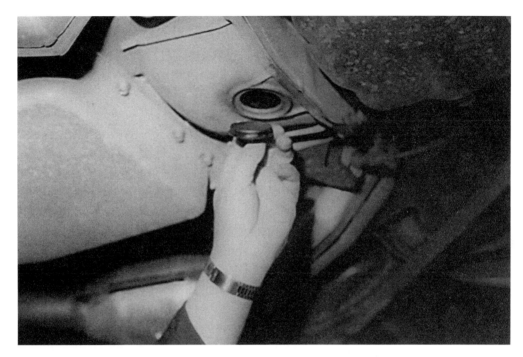

FIGURE 138
The torque converter is the bell-shaped housing that is part of an automatic
transmission. Some have inspection and drain plugs; others do not.

COMPONENT: **Body**

PROBLEM: **Unwanted stickers on bumpers and body panels**

This repair is done in two steps: (1) removing the sticker, and (2) removing the film of adhesive that remains.

Proceed as follows:

1. Hold a hair dryer set on high heat about 12 inches from the sticker and turn the dryer on.
2. Move the nozzle of the dryer back and forth across the face of the sticker to soften the adhesive.
3. Starting in a corner, pull gently to peel off the sticker. Keep the dryer moving so that heat does not concentrate in one spot for too long, which may damage paint.
4. If the sticker clings tightly, you may have to scrape it off. Wrap the metal edge of a putty knife with duct tape. Heat the face of the sticker with the hair dryer for about 90 seconds. Then, scrape the sticker off with the putty knife as you continue to apply heat.
5. When the sticker has been removed, dampen a soft rag with rubbing alcohol and wipe the bumper or body panel to remove residue left by adhesive.
6. Wet a rag with water, scoop a dab of polishing compound onto the rag, and rub the spot gently. Then, wash the bumper or panel with water from a hose, wipe it dry, and apply a coat of auto wax to complete the repair.

COMPONENT: **Body**

PROBLEM: **Baked-on wax**

If you apply wax to the body of a car that is sitting in sunlight and fail to rub the wax off immediately, the sun will bake the wax to the body. Here is how to remove it without damaging the finish:

Buy a photographer's sponge from a photo supply store. This soft material won't streak the finish as will the sponges you buy in a supermarket.

Saturate the sponge with undiluted liquid laundry detergent. With the sponge dripping wet, rub the body of the vehicle. Treat one small section at a time and immediately flood that section with water from a garden hose. Don't allow the detergent to dry. This should remove the wax; if some remains, repeat the procedure.

COMPONENT: **Body**

PROBLEM: **Vehicle doesn't come clean; rust**

You can wash a vehicle by taking it through an automatic car wash or by hand-washing it. Hand-washing is more effective for removing dirt and film-forming residue.

You will need a nondetergent soap, such as Murphy Oil Soap™. Do not use a liquid or powdered laundry detergent. Such products can harm paint. You will also need a large, soft car-washing sponge with open pores, as well as a chamois. Both items are available from an auto supply store.

Follow these steps:

1. Connect a garden hose and spray the underside of the body and the insides (wells) of fenders with heavy blasts of water to wash away road salt, which is corrosive and can cause rust.
2. Inspect the body for rust spots, especially quarter panels and fender wells. Use a penknife to scrape off rust, and spray the spot with rustproofing compound, which is sold in aerosol cans at auto supply stores. It is important to eliminate rust when it's in a formative state. If the condition is allowed to spread, an expensive repair by a professional body shop can be anticipated.
3. Park the car in shade.
4. Mix car-wash soap in a bucket of warm water to make a sudsy solution.
5. Wash the car from the top down, one section at a time. Start with the roof, followed by the hood, deck lid, each side, grille, and the rear panel. Using the sponge, flood the section with the soapy solution, pressing down to loosen grime. Before the solution has a chance to dry, spray the section with water from a garden hose. Move on to the next section.
6. After the car has been washed, spray it with water again. Then, dry it with the chamois, but first soak the chamois in water and wring it out. Start with the roof and proceed from section to section. As the chamois becomes saturated, wring it out.
7. Finally, inspect the body for tar and insect residue, which can be removed with a tar-and-bug solvent.

COMPONENT: **Body**

PROBLEM: **Faded paint**

The paint on a vehicle is affected by the ultraviolet rays of the sun. In time, paint fades, but this doesn't mean that the car has to be repainted. Paint is applied to a vehicle in layers. Removing the top layer of faded paint exposes the like-new paint that lies beneath it.

Several products are available for removing faded paint. Selecting the product that is best suited to the particular type of paint on your vehicle is of utmost importance. If you select the wrong product, you could rub off all the layers of paint, exposing the gray primer coat.

Products fall into three categories: compounds, cleaner-waxes, and polishes.

Compounds and cleaner-waxes contain abrasives. Cleaner-wax has a minimum amount of abrasive, polishing compound (not to be confused with polish) has more, and rubbing compound has the most. Rubbing compound is used only when the paint on the vehicle is in such bad condition that if it fails to do the job, there is no alternative but to repaint the car.

Polish contains no abrasives. It possesses a cleaner that will remove dirt but not faded paint.

The first step in selecting a product is to identify the type of paint on the vehicle. There are three categories of paint. The following describes each type of paint, which product to use, and ways to use it.

> **NOTE**   If you don't know what type of paint is on your car and such information is not in the owner's manual, ask the service department manager at a dealership that sells your make of vehicle.

Clearcoat/Basecoat Paint

Pigmented paint is used for the bottom coat. This is called the basecoat. The top coats of paint contain no pigment. They are transparent, which is why they are called the clearcoat. The clearcoat protects the basecoat from the sun's rays and keeps it from getting dirty. In fact, just washing the vehicle, especially by hand (see page 144), will remove dirt from the clearcoat to allow the luster of the basecoat to show through.

In time, however, the top layer of clearcoat can fade. Removing this layer will expose the layer beneath it.

Clearcoat layers are comparatively thin, so you must proceed with caution when dealing with basecoat/clearcoat paint. When washing no longer produces a satisfactory result, first try to restore the luster of paint with a polish, which is nonabrasive and will not remove paint. If this fails to produce the desired effect, step up to a cleaner-wax, which is mildly abrasive, and then, if necessary, to a more abrasive polishing compound. Rubbing compound should not be used on a clearcoat/basecoat paint; it will rub right through the clearcoat layers.

Apply any product with a light hand. Don't use heavy pressure or a machine. Doing so will cause all the clearcoat to be rubbed off.

Metallic Paint

Use a polish specifically formulated for metallic paint. Do not use an abrasive product.

Enamel or Lacquer Nonmetallic Paint

To restore the luster of a nonmetallic, nonbasecoat/clearcoat paint job, use polishing compound. If that proves unsatisfactory, use rubbing compound.

Whichever product you use—polish, cleaner-wax, or compound— the best result is attained by first hand-washing the vehicle as described on page 138. Try to do the job on a cloudy day. If this is not possible, park the car in shade.

Apply the product to one section at a time, the area of which should not exceed two square feet. Use a circular motion if the product is nonabrasive, a back-and-forth motion if it is abrasive. If an applicator is not provided with the product, use a terry-cloth rag. Read the manufacturer instructions on the container to find out whether the applicator should be damp or dry. Use clean terry-cloth rags to remove the product before it hardens. Then, buff the surface with another clean rag.

When applying an abrasive product near the edges of doors, fenders, hood, and trunk lid, use no pressure. Otherwise, you may rub off the paint, which is thinnest at these points.

The following measures will help you obtain satisfactory results when using an abrasive product:

1. Cover moldings and hood ornaments with masking tape.
2. To remove deep scratches in the paint that may be revealed after the faded paint has been removed, saturate a piece of 600- or 800-grit sandpaper with water and rub the scratch using light pressure. Then, wash the area with water from a garden hose.

3. If the paint still appears dull after the initial treatment, more of the faded layer needs to be removed. Repeat the treatment.
4. After the paint's luster has been restored, wax the vehicle. Wax protects paint from the sun's rays. It does not make the vehicle "shine." Contrary to popular belief, applying more than one coat of wax is a waste of time. In applying a second coat, you will only rub off the first.

COMPONENT: Body

PROBLEM: **Surface scratches and isolated chips in paint**

A surface scratch or isolated chip in paint can usually be eliminated.

SCRATCHES. First try polishing compound.

CAUTION

Do not do this if your vehicle has metallic paint.

Fold a soft cloth into a pad. Dip the pad into water, wring it out, and scoop a small dab of compound onto the cloth. Then, rub the scratch using straight back-and-forth strokes. Do *not* press.

After four or five passes over the damaged spot, wipe the area with a soft, dry rag. If the scratch is still visible, repeat the procedure once more. Further treatment with polishing compound is not recommended, because too much paint will be removed. Instead, touch up the scratch as described below.

CHIPS. To get rid of an isolated chip or stubborn scratch, use a touch-up paint that matches the color of the paint on your car, as follows:

1. If the spot has started to rust, scrape rust off with the tip of a pocketknife.
2. To make the repair using touch-up paint that comes in a jar, shake the jar to mix the paint; then, unscrew the cap. A small brush should be attached to the cap. If not, buy a natural-bristle artist's brush of suitable size from an art supply store. Dab a small amount of touch-up paint onto the chip or scratch. Use several fine strokes to blend the paint with the finish of the car.
3. If using touch-up paint that comes in a spray can, do *not* spray the paint directly from the can onto the damaged area. Doing so will probably result in overspray onto adjacent surfaces, entailing messy cleanup. Instead, shake the can to mix the paint and spray some into the cap of the can (Figure 139). Let the paint thicken. Then, dip a small wooden stick, such as the nonsulfur end of a kitchen match, into the paint and apply it to the chip (Figures 140 and 141).

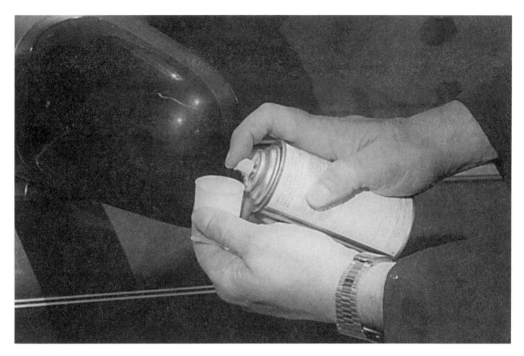

FIGURE 139
Spray the paint into the cap of the paint can.

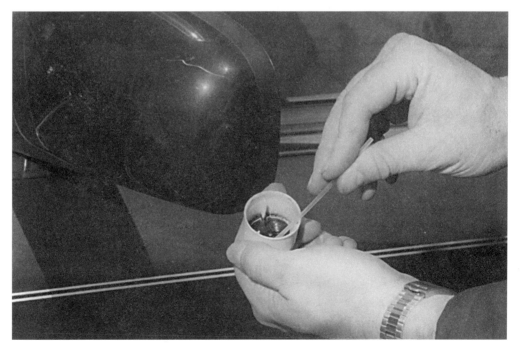

FIGURE 140
Dip a small stick into the paint after allowing time for the paint to thicken.

143

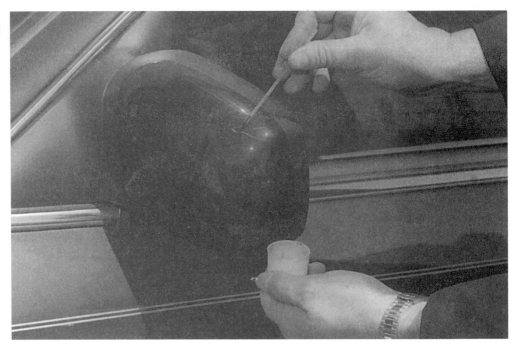

FIGURE 141
Spread the paint over the scratch.

COMPONENT: **Body**

PROBLEM: **Deep scratches and numerous chips in paint**

The repair described here assumes the presence of deep scratches and numerous chips spread over the paint of a body panel, making the repair described above ineffective. It also assumes the unavailability of a compressor and paint gun. The purpose of making the following repairs yourself, therefore, is to reduce costs by doing preparatory work before turning the car over to an auto body paint shop for repainting.

You will need these supplies: wax-removing solvent; a sanding block; a tack cloth; 80-, 240-, and 400-grit sandpaper; glazing putty; spray cans of zinc chromate and finishing primer; and a rubber contour squeegee.

Here is what to do:

1. After washing and drying the body panel, clean it with wax-removing solvent.
2. Use 80-grit sandpaper attached to the sanding block over the damaged area. Keep the sanding block flat against the surface and apply moderate pressure. Move the sandpaper in a back-and-forth motion. Do this until you produce bare metal. Then, wipe the area clean.
3. Using a piece of 240-grit sandpaper attached to the sanding block, sand the area again to remove scratches in the metal that were made by the 80-grit sandpaper.
4. The next sanding step is done to get the area as smooth as possible. Use 400-grit sandpaper attached to the sanding block. Keep the sandpaper wet.
5. After sanding, wash the area with plain water and wipe it with the tack cloth, which will remove fine particles.
6. Let the surface dry completely.
7. Cover moldings and adjacent panels with newspaper held in place with masking tape. This is done to guard against primer overspray.
8. Hold the spray can of zinc chromate primer parallel to the area, at a distance of 10 to 12 inches. Moving the can back and forth, spray the primer onto the surface until all bare metal is covered.
9. Let the primer dry.
10. Scoop a glob of glazing putty onto the edges of a rubber contour squeegee and spread it onto the surface. Use moderate pressure so that the putty will stick. Move the squeegee in one direction only.

11. After the putty dries, sand it with 240-grit sandpaper attached to the sanding block. Sand until the putty is level with the surrounding surface. Run your hand over the area to make certain no high spots remain. Then, inspect the putty for the presence of pits or rough areas and to determine whether you inadvertently sanded off too much, leaving a low spot. If necessary, apply another layer of glazing putty and repeat the sanding operation.

12. Attach 800-grit sandpaper to the sanding block, saturate the paper with water, and sand the repaired area of the panel until the surface is as smooth as possible. Dip the sandpaper into water frequently.

13. When you are satisfied with the smoothness of the panel, wash it and then wipe it with the tack cloth. Let the surface dry completely.

14. Apply the finish primer, using the same technique described for application of the zinc chromate primer. The panel is now ready for painting.

COMPONENT: **Body**

PROBLEM: **Faded black plastic trim**

The high-gloss black plastic that is used as trim and on bumpers has a tendency to dull as it ages. The following procedure may restore its luster:

1. Wash and dry the trim.
2. Scrub the trim with an old toothbrush that you have dipped into an automotive vinyl cleaner, such as Armor All™, which is available from auto supply stores. This is done to remove wax.
3. If step 2 doesn't restore trim to its original appearance, mix together three parts of mineral spirits to one part of rubbing alcohol.

   Select an inconspicuous spot and rub it with an old toothbrush dipped into the mixture. Then, wash the spot and let it dry to determine whether the mixture further dulls the trim. If it does, you will have to be satisfied with the trim or have it repainted. If the mixture brightens the spot, use it to treat the entire piece of trim.
4. Spray a polish specifically designed for black plastic trim, such as STP Sun-of-a-Gun™ or Clear Guard™, onto a clean rag. Rub it onto the trim to restore luster. Repeat the application until the trim's appearance is satisfactory.
5. Coat the trim with a protective agent, such as Black Again™, 3M Scotchgard Protective Gel™, and Black Chrome™.

COMPONENT: Body

PROBLEM: Door won't close

If the door of your car doesn't close properly, first make sure that it is not being blocked by a safety belt or some other item. Then, move the door handle in and out a few times to try and rotate the door latch back into position. If this fails, hold the door handle in the open position and rotate the latch down into the closed position using the tip of a screwdriver (Figure 142).

A door latch that continues to hang up should be treated with a silicone lubricant, such as WD-40. Hold the end of the applicator that comes with the product in the groove formed by the top of the latch and the edge of the door frame. Give it one squirt (Figure 143). Activate the door handle a few times to spread the lubricant.

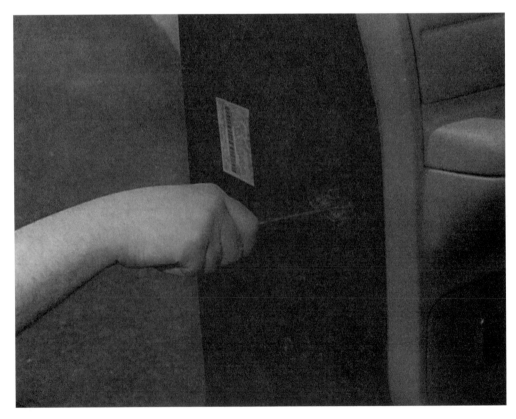

FIGURE 142
A door won't close if the latch sticks. Press the latch down using a screwdriver.

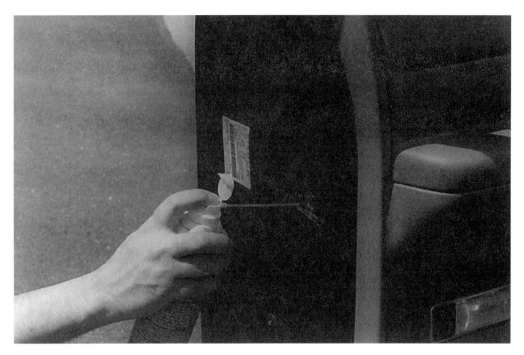

FIGURE 143
Squirt some silicone onto the latch mechanism.

COMPONENT: **Body**

PROBLEM: **Water leak under dash; blocked drain holes that trap water, causing rust**

A water leak that shows up under the dash soon after a windshield is replaced is caused by caulking compound used for the repair that fills the drain holes along the bottom of the windshield channel. Water that normally would drain through these openings and fall harmlessly to the ground will instead run down the bulkhead and find its way into the vehicle.

Small drain openings are also present along the bottoms of doors (Figure 144). If they become blocked with rustproofing compound, water will remain trapped inside the door and can cause rust.

If your situation fits one of these scenarios, use a pointed tool, such as an awl, to probe and clean each opening.

FIGURE 144
Doors possess holes through which water can drain. These must be kept unobstructed to prevent rust.

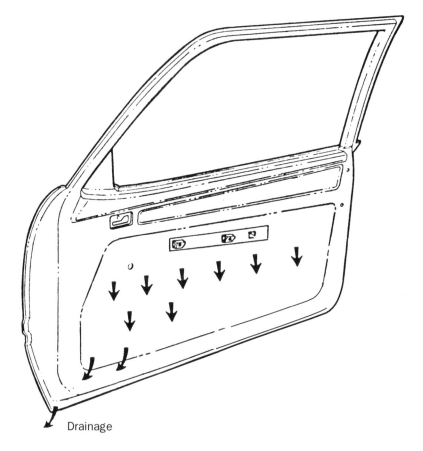

Drainage

COMPONENT: Body

PROBLEM: **Squeak from a door; squeak or bang from below**

Do you hear an annoying squeak from around one or more doors when your car goes over bumps? Weatherstripping may have lost resiliency and begun rubbing. Here is what to do:

1. Clean weatherstripping with a rag moistened with a household cleaner, such as Fantastik™, Glass Plus™, or Windex™.
2. Allow the cleaner to evaporate, or wipe it off.
3. Restore resiliency to weatherstripping by applying 3M Liquid Silicone Plus™, Armor All™, or STP Sun-of-a-Gun™. Use an amount that leaves the material looking slightly wet. Do not wipe off the lubricant. If the squeak persists, apply more.

If you hear a squeak or bang from under the car, it may be coming from a loose exhaust system component, such as the tailpipe. Tighten the supports, called hangers, that hold these parts (Figure 145).

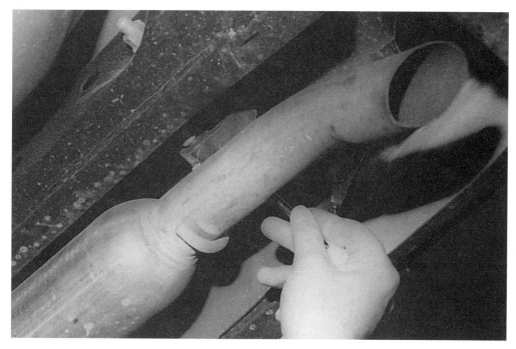

FIGURE 145
Tightening the bolts of exhaust system hangers will frequently get rid of an annoying squeak or banging sound coming from under the body.

COMPONENT: **Body**

PROBLEM: **Wind noise and water leaks**

If weatherstripping tears, becomes separated from its channel, or wears out, a water leak and/or wind noise from around a door may occur.

To determine whether noise is coming from one of the doors, use two-inch-wide duct tape to seal the seam between the body of the vehicle and one of the doors (Figure 146). Drive the car. If the noise has disappeared, the weatherstripping around that door should be treated as described below. On the other hand, if the wind noise is still there, strip off the duct tape, seal another door, and repeat the test.

To determine whether defective weatherstripping is responsible for water leaking into the vehicle, aim a garden hose at the door nearest the spot where water is found. Stand about three feet away and spray the seams between the door and the body for at least 15 minutes. Check to see whether there is water in the vehicle. Then, move on to a section that hasn't been sprayed. You have to be patient. It can take a while for water to work its way into the vehicle through a gap in the weatherstripping.

FIGURE 146
To determine whether a wind noise is coming from a door, seal the seams around the door with tape.

When it becomes obvious that air or water is leaking around a door, inspect weatherstripping for tears. Repair a slit with silicone rubber sealant (Figure 147), which is available from hardware stores.

To determine whether weatherstripping has separated from its channel, pull gently on the piece over its entire length. If weatherstripping comes out of the channel, wipe the channel clean with a rag and apply rubber cement or liquid butyl sealer to the underside of the weatherstripping and to the channel (Figure 148). Then, press the weatherstripping back into the channel. To put pressure on the weatherstripping until it adheres to the channel, use spring-type wooden or plastic clothespins as clamps (Figure 149). Place the clothespins one inch apart.

To determine whether weatherstripping has simply worn out, place a crisp dollar bill at a spot on the weatherstripping and close the door. Try to pull the dollar free (Figure 150). If there is no resistance, weatherstripping is worn in that spot. Be sure to test the entire length of weatherstripping.

If weatherstripping is worn, pull it out of the channel. Clean the channel with a solvent. If you discover rust, scrape it off with the tip of a penknife. Then, lay a length of double-sided polyethylene foam tape in the channel. This product is available from auto parts and hardware stores.

FIGURE 147
A slit in weatherstripping can be repaired with a silicone rubber sealant, such as this one sold by Ford.

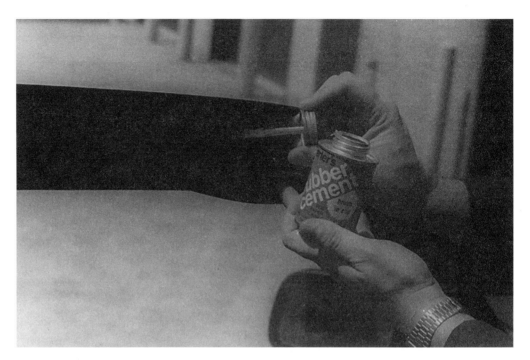

FIGURE 148
To resecure a length of loose weatherstripping, spread rubber cement on the backside of the strip and on the channel.

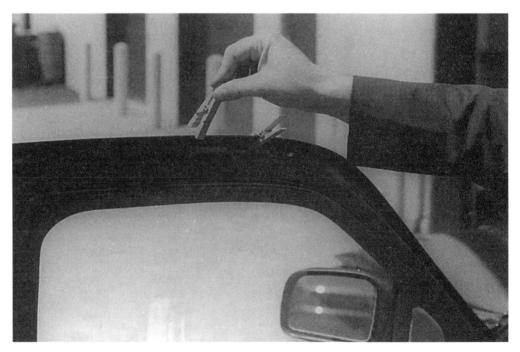

FIGURE 149
Use clothespins to clamp the weatherstrip to the channel.

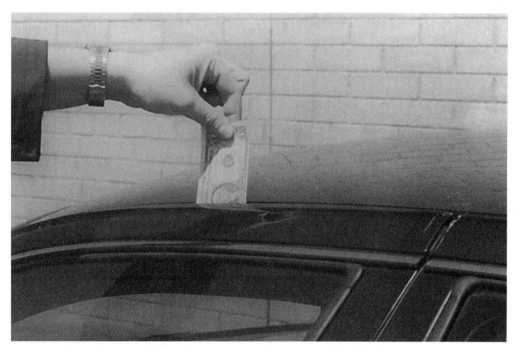

FIGURE 150
Use a dollar bill to determine whether weatherstripping is worn and should be replaced.

Dampen a rag with mineral spirits or rubbing alcohol and wipe down the underside of the weatherstripping. After it is dry, press the weatherstripping back into the channel. The thickness provided by the double-sided polyethylene foam tape will compensate for the wear that has taken place.

COMPONENT: **Body**

PROBLEM: **Frozen door locks**

One of the following methods can be used to unlock the doors of a vehicle if locks freeze:

1. Grasp the key with pliers. Heat it with a match for several seconds. When the key is hot, quickly insert it into the keyhole. The warmth from the key will be transferred to the lock cylinder and cause ice to melt.
2. If an electric outlet is available and you have a hair dryer handy, turn the dryer on high heat. Aim the nozzle at the lock to melt the ice.
3. To guard against being locked out while on the road, keep a squirt can of lock deicer in your car. You can buy it from an auto parts store or a locksmith. A few squirts into the keyway will free the lock (Figure 151). Obviously, if you forget to take the can out of the glove compartment when you leave and lock the car, it won't do you any good.

FIGURE 151
A shot or two of de-icer will melt ice in a door keyway.

COMPONENT: **Body**

PROBLEM: **Key broken off in a lock**

To retrieve a key that has broken off in a lock, grind or file the flat side of a coping saw blade until the blade is half its original width. Insert the blade into the keyhole with the teeth of the blade facing up so that they will engage the teeth of the broken-off key (Figure 152). When the blade locks on to the key, draw the key out of the keyway until you can grasp the end with a pair of needle-nose pliers. Pull the key out of the lock.

If you don't have a duplicate key, take the two broken pieces to a locksmith, who can use them to make you a new one.

FIGURE 152
Use a coping saw blade to retrieve a key that breaks off in a lock.

COMPONENT: **Body**

PROBLEM: **Hole in carpeting**

A hole burned into the carpet of a vehicle by a smoker can be repaired as follows:

1. Using a utility knife and manicure scissors, cut and scrape away burned fibers and scorched cloth.
2. Loosen the molding from a door sill and pull the edge of the carpet free (Figure 153).
3. Use scissors to cut fibers from the edge of the carpet (Figure 154). Don't tuck the edge of the carpet back under the molding just yet. You may need more fibers.
4. Spray a thin layer of carpet and fiber adhesive into the spot where the burn occurred. Make sure to cover the entire spot. You can buy carpet and fiber adhesive from a hardware store. Tell the salesperson what you are doing to make sure you get the correct product.

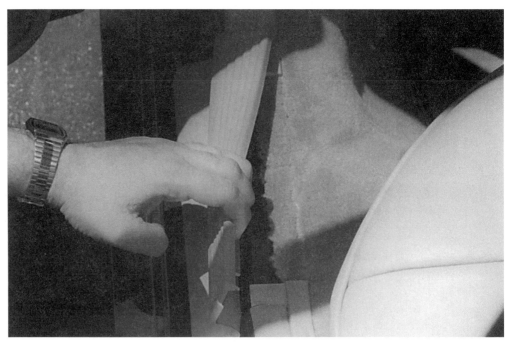

FIGURE 153
The trim molding that hides the edge of carpeting in some cars is secured by screws that can be removed. In this particular car, molding snaps into a groove. To release this style of molding, grasp the edge and pull it back.

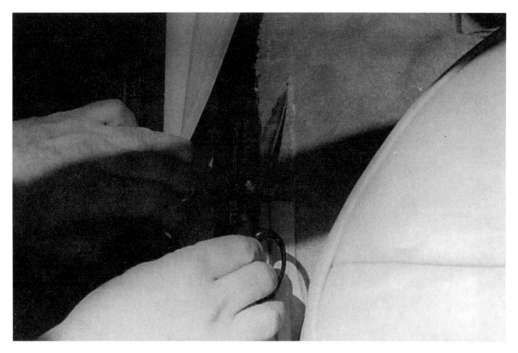

FIGURE 154
Cut off fibers needed to fill the hole left by the burn.

5. Using tweezers, pick up one fiber at a time and carefully place it upright into the adhesive so the fiber doesn't fall over. Work from the outside of the spot toward the center. Fill the hole with enough fibers to obtain a density equal to the surrounding carpet. Allow time (two or three days) for the fibers to adhere.

COMPONENT: **Coolant**

PROBLEM: **Disappearance from the coolant tank**

If coolant mysteriously disappears from the coolant tank, the tank or the hose that connects the tank to the radiator is probably leaking (Figures 155 and 156). The location of the leak is often not apparent until you remove the tank for closer examination, as follows:

CAUTION

Make sure the engine is cold. Wear work gloves.

---

1. Remove from the coolant tank the cap that holds one end of the hose. Pull the other end of the hose off the fitting on the radiator (Figure 157).

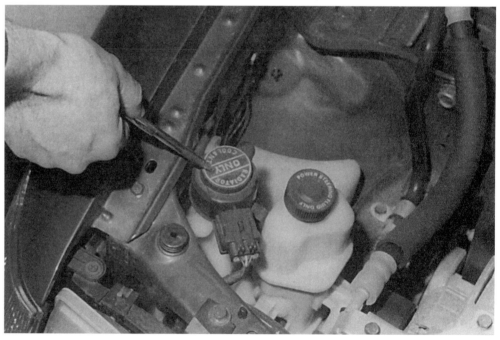

FIGURE 155
If coolant disappears from the coolant tank, the tank or the hose is probably leaking.

FIGURE 156
The hose runs from the tank to the radiator. Coolant flows back and forth between the two through the hose.

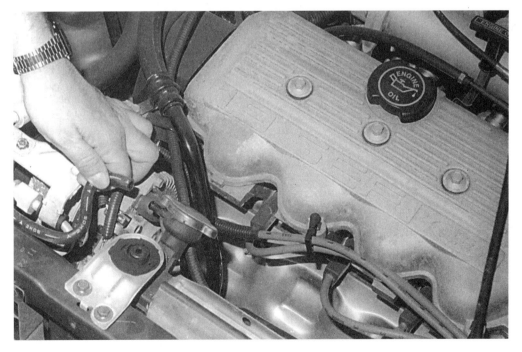

FIGURE 157
With the engine cold, disconnect the hose and examine its surface for damage.

2. Inspect the hose by squeezing it. This will reveal any split. Replace the hose if damaged.

3. Undo the fastener(s) that holds the tank and take the tank out of the engine compartment. This may require removal of another component that blocks the tank (Figures 158 and 159).

4. Discard any coolant remaining in the tank.

5. Fill the empty tank with water and inspect it for leakage. If there is a leak, buy a new tank from an auto parts store. You could, however, keep the old tank in service by inserting a gallon-size plastic freezer bag into the tank. Tie the top of the bag to the fill hole of the tank.

6. Install the tank and fill it to the FULL COLD mark with the proper mixture of ethylene glycol and water needed to meet the lowest ambient temperature anticipated for your region (see page 105).

FIGURE 158
In this car, the coolant tank is jammed behind the power-steering fluid tank. If the coolant tank must be replaced, the power-steering fluid tank first has to be moved out of the way.

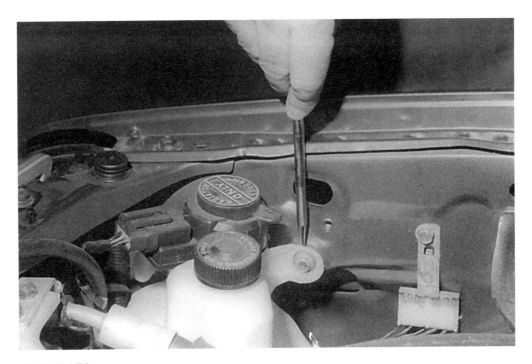

FIGURE 159
To release the power-steering fluid tank, loosen the bolt. Note that the caps of both tanks are distinctively marked as to what goes in each. Pay close attention to this. You don't want coolant in the power-steering tank or power-steering fluid in the coolant tank.

COMPONENT: Drive belt(s)

PROBLEM: Noise

A squeak, squeal, or chirp that is heard from the engine may be coming from a drive belt. Engines have either one long belt or two or more shorter belts.

A drive belt or belts wrap around a pulley that is attached to the engine crankshaft and around other pulleys that are attached to various engine components, such as the cooling fan, water pump, air conditioner compressor, A/C generator, and power steering pump. As the crankshaft pulley drives the belts, they, in turn, drive components.

Heat given off by the engine can eventually cause a belt to dry out and lose elasticity. The belt will then rub against pulleys, creating the squeak, chirp, or squeal.

The simple repair described below may allow you to silence a dry belt that is making noise. If it doesn't, replace the belt as described on page 166. First, twist the belt along its entire length to determine whether it is cracked, frayed at the edges, covered with oil, or glazed. A glazed belt has a shiny appearance. Replace a belt that exhibits any of these characteristics.

If the engine has a single belt (referred to as a serpentine belt) that seems to be in sound condition, lubricate it with a silicone spray such as WD-40™ (Figure 160).

If the engine has multiple belts (called V-belts because of the shape they take when wrapped around their respective pulleys), use a lubricant called "belt dressing," which is available from auto supply stores. With the engine turned off, spray belts and pulleys with the lubricant. Start the engine and let it run at idle speed for a minute or two to spread lubricant over surfaces you were unable to reach.

CAUTION

Keep away from belts and the cooling fan when the engine is running.

FIGURE 160
Spraying a serpentine drive belt with a silicone lubricant may stop it from squeaking.

COMPONENT: Drive belt(s)

PROBLEM: Damage

The repairs described here are for loose or damaged engine belts and for those that remain noisy even after the repair described on page 164.

A V-belt that stretches and becomes loose can reduce the output of the A/C generator, resulting in a run-down battery. It may also result in overheating and affect the power steering. V-belts should not "give" more than ½ inch when you press on the longest span of the belt with your thumb midway between two pulleys.

> **NOTE** A one-piece serpentine belt doesn't need to be adjusted manually, because it has an automatic adjusting mechanism.

To tighten a V-belt, loosen the bolt that secures the bracket of the accessory it serves (Figure 161).

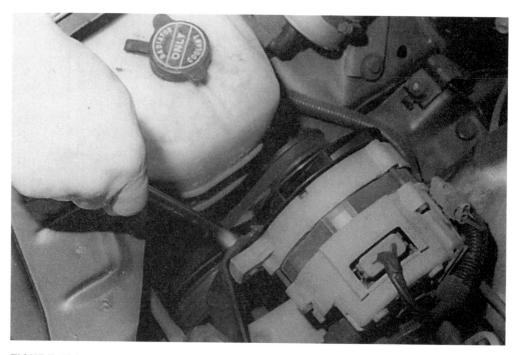

FIGURE 161
To adjust (or remove) a V-belt, loosen the bracket of the accessory the belt serves—in this case, the A/C generator.

Tighten the accessory to tighten the belt (Figure 162). Check with your thumb as described above and stop tightening when the belt has a slack of $\frac{1}{4}$ to $\frac{1}{2}$ inch. If leverage is needed to get the belt tight enough, place a pry bar against a solid metal part of the accessory to draw the belt tighter. Then, tighten the mounting bolt.

To replace a V-belt that is cracked, frayed, oil-covered, or glazed, loosen the mounting bolt of the particular accessory bracket and push the accessory in toward the engine until the belt is slack enough to be removed. If another belt is in the way, it will have to be removed first.

To install a new V-belt, wrap it around its pulleys. Then, pull back on the particular accessory to tighten the belt until the "thumb test" shows that the belt has a slack of $\frac{1}{4}$ to $\frac{1}{2}$ inch. Tighten the mounting bolt.

To replace a serpentine belt, look for the automatic adjusting mechanism. Tension on the belt is released by inserting a pry bar into the slotted tab in the automatic adjusting mechanism (Figures 163 and 164). Push against the mechanism with the pry bar, which relieves tension on the belt (Figure 165). Remove the belt from the engine (Figure 166).

FIGURE 162
Tighten the accessory to tighten the belt. A pry bar may be needed. When the belt is adjusted, tighten the bracket bolt.

NOTE Before removing a serpentine belt, make a sketch of how the belt wraps around each of the pulleys, so you will have no doubts about installing the new belt (Figures 167 and 168).

After installing the new serpentine belt, release pressure on the automatic adjuster. This puts the necessary tension on the belt.

IMPORTANT

V-belts and serpentine belts come in a variety of sizes. Make sure you get the correct size belt for your engine. Do this by describing the engine to the salesperson at the auto supply store or by bringing along the old belt.

FIGURE 163
To release a serpentine belt, look for a slot such as this one in the arm of the automatic adjusting mechanism.

Automatic adjusting mechanism

FIGURE 164
Insert a pry bar into the slot.

FIGURE 165
Pushing down releases the belt.

FIGURE 166
Remove the belt.

FIGURE 167
Before removing a serpentine belt, make a sketch of how the belt wraps around each pulley.

FIGURE 168
Use the sketch to install a new belt. Obviously, wrapping the belt improperly will cause a problem.

COMPONENT: **Heater**

PROBLEM: **Lack of heat**

To determine whether it is taking too long for your vehicle's heater to give off sufficient heat, use a kitchen thermometer (the type placed in roasted meat to measure internal temperature). Insert the probe of the thermometer into a heating vent, start the engine, and turn heater controls to maximum output. Consult the owner's manual to verify that you are setting controls correctly.

If the engine is cold, it will take about three minutes for the thermometer to begin registering. The thermometer should record 100°F or more in less than five minutes. If it doesn't, wait for the engine to get cold again. Then, remove the radiator cap, insert the thermometer into the coolant, and start the engine. The thermometer should record a temperature of 180°F or more within three minutes. If it doesn't, the reason for inadequate heater performance lies with the cooling system thermostat, which should be replaced as explained on page 10.

If the temperature of the coolant reaches 180°F within three minutes, the heater may be clogged. Turn off the engine, remove the thermometer, and put the cap back on the radiator.

CAUTION

Be careful not to touch the engine or radiator. They will be hot enough to burn you.

To determine whether the heater core is clogged, run the engine at idle and turn on the heater. Now, *carefully* place one hand on each of the heater hoses. If both are warm, but one (the outlet hose) is warmer than the other (the inlet hose), the reason for lack of heat lies with a faulty control system or heater doors that aren't opening. Consult a mechanic.

If both hoses are cool, or if the outlet hose is cold while the inlet hose is warm, the cause of the problem is probably a clogged heater. You may have to have the heater replaced. Then again, the following repair may work:

1. Wait for the engine to get cold.
2. Disconnect both heater hoses at the heater and attach them so that the outlet hose is on the side normally occupied by the inlet hose and the inlet hose is on the side normally occupied by the outlet hose.

3. Drive the vehicle for several days with the heater turned on.

4. With the engine cold, reconnect hoses to their original positions. Does the heater now provide heat? If so, what you did by reversing hoses was to reverse the flow of coolant through the heater, which dislodged debris in the core that was causing the blockage.

If the repair fails, try one more trick before consulting a mechanic. Buy three feet of heater hose from an auto supply store. Cut the hose in half to produce two 18-inch pieces. Wait for the engine to get cold and disconnect the heater hoses. Attach one of the pieces to the inlet fitting of the heater core and the other to the outlet fitting.

Buy a garden-hose adapter from a hardware store. Connect this to the open end of the hose that is attached to the outlet side of the heater core. Turn the heater on and set it for maximum heat. Do *not* start the engine.

Now, attach a garden hose to the garden-hose adapter. Turn the faucet on full force for 30 seconds and turn it off for five seconds. Repeat this five times.

Switch the garden-hose adapter and garden hose to the hose on the inlet fitting of the heater core to flush that side. This may dislodge whatever is clogging the heater core.

After switching the garden-hose adapter and garden hose back and forth between the outlet and inlet sides three times each, and flushing the heater core each time, reattach the regular heater hoses and test to see whether you have succeeded in breaking the blockage. If not, you may want to perform the flushing procedure another time or two before giving it up as a lost cause.

COMPONENT: **Lights**

PROBLEM: **Burned-out halogen headlight**

Most vehicles manufactured since the mid-1980s are equipped with halogen bulbs. If the bulb burns out, it can usually be replaced without replacing the entire headlight unit, because the bulb and headlight are separate. This is different from a sealed-beam headlight, where the lighting filament (bulb) and the lens are integrated into a single unit. With a sealed-beam system, the entire unit must be replaced if the filament burns out.

One way to determine whether your car is equipped with halogen or conventional sealed-beam headlights is to examine the trim around the headlights. If there are no screws, you have halogen bulbs.

A halogen bulb is more expensive than a conventional sealed-beam headlight. However, it provides a brighter beam and usually lasts for a longer time. Halogen bulbs are also easier to replace when they burn out.

Follow these steps:

1. Open the hood and look at the back end of the burned-out bulb. You will see a serrated locking ring, which is the bulb socket (Figure 169).
2. Turn the ring to release the socket and bulb (Figure 170). Usually, the ring must be twisted $1/4$ turn to the left.
3. Holding the socket in one hand and the plastic bulb holder in the other, pull the two apart.
4. Buy a new halogen bulb of the same designation as the old bulb.

C A U T I O N

Do *not* touch the glass of the new halogen bulb with your bare hands or allow it to come in contact with any dirty surface. Dirt and body oil transferred to the glass surface will cause a halogen bulb to fail prematurely. Hold the bulb by the plastic terminal housing.

---

5. Insert the new bulb into the socket (Figure 171). Make sure they lock.

FIGURE 169
A halogen headlight bulb is replaced from inside the engine compartment. A sealed-beam headlight is replaced from the outside (see Figures 172 to 177).

FIGURE 170
Turning the serrated ring, which is the socket, releases the halogen assembly.

Socket

FIGURE 171
In handling a halogen assembly, do not touch the bulb. Place your hand on the plastic holder.

6. Line up the socket and bulb with the opening in the lens and push it in until you are able to engage the serrated locking ring.
7. Turn the ring (usually to the right) to lock the halogen bulb and socket in the lens.

COMPONENT: **Lights**

PROBLEM: **Burned-out sealed-beam headlight; corroded headlight socket**

To replace a burned-out sealed-beam headlight, follow these steps:

1. Examine the trim around the headlight to determine whether screws are of the cross-slotted Phillips-head or star-shaped Torx variety. If they are Torx screws, you will need a Torx driver, which can be purchased from an auto parts store.
2. Remove the screws and take off the trim (Figures 172 and 173).
3. You will see several screws around the sealed-beam unit. One or two of them will have small springs, which are used to adjust the headlight beam (Figure 174). Do not turn them; if you do, the light will have to be readjusted. The other screws hold the unit in place. Remove them (Figure 175).

FIGURE 172
Remove screws securing the trim.

FIGURE 173
Take off the trim.

FIGURE 174
Examine screws before turning them to find those used for adjusting the beam of the headlight. Do not turn these.

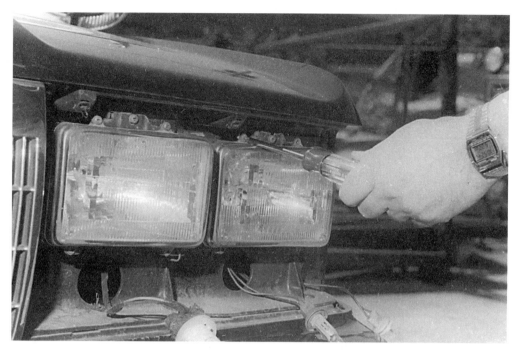

FIGURE 175
Remove only those screws that keep the sealed-beam unit in place.

IMPORTANT

If screws are corroded and won't budge, don't force them. Squirt them with a liberal dose of penetrating oil and wait at least 15 minutes. The screws should now come free. If they don't, give them another shot of penetrating oil.

---

4. Draw the sealed-beam unit out of the housing and grasp the socket (Figure 176). Then, pull the burned-out unit from the socket (Figure 177).
5. Buy a new sealed-beam unit of the same type as the burned-out unit.
6. Before plugging the new unit into the socket, spray electric contact cleaner into the socket openings to eliminate corrosion. A socket that is corroded can shorten the life of a sealed-beam unit. You can buy this cleaner from an electronics supply or hardware

FIGURE 176
Pull out the burned-out headlight until you can grasp the socket on the back of the unit.

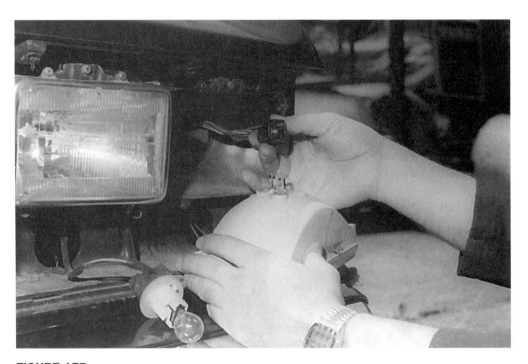

FIGURE 177
Pull the socket from the terminals, discard the old headlight, and plug a new unit into the socket.

store. Then, press the terminals of the sealed-beam unit into the socket.

7. Align the retaining tabs of the new headlight with the retaining screw holes in the housing and install the unit. Engage retaining screws and tighten them just enough to hold the unit in place.

8. Replace and secure the trim ring.

COMPONENT: Lights

PROBLEM: Broken taillight lens; burned-out rear bulb

Depending on the extent of the damage, there are several ways to repair a taillight lens. You can seal a crack without removing the lens by using an instant glue such as Zap Gap™, which is available from hobby and craft shops.

If the lens is shattered, you can use lens repair tape, which is available from auto supply stores. The result isn't particularly attractive, but the tape will prevent water from getting into the socket, causing corrosion and ruining the light.

The advantage to repairing damage with tape is that you don't have to remove the lens. However, by removing it you can make a neater repair with Form-a-Lens™, which is available from auto supply stores. This repair compound is a plastic material that closely resembles and blends with the lens. Here is how to use it:

1. If the taillight lens contains ridges, use modeling clay to make a mold before removing the lens. Do this by spreading clay over a part of the lens that is intact. Press the clay down to imprint the lens ridges into the clay. Peel off the mold carefully so as not to disrupt the impression.

> **NOTE** If the taillight has no ridges, you don't have to make a clay mold.

2. Remove the broken lens from the vehicle (Figure 178). If assembly screws aren't visible on the face of the lens, look in the luggage compartment or on the underside of the bumper. This also is the case if you have to remove a parking lens to replace a burned-out taillight or rear turn-signal bulb or to replace a cracked lens.
3. Once the lens has been removed, clean it with a mixture of water and vinegar or with window cleaner. Then, dry it.
4. Cover the face of the broken section of lens with the clear plastic film that comes in the repair kit if the lens has no ridges. For a lens with ridges, cover the face of the broken section with the clay mold.
5. After mixing the plastic repair compound according to the instructions supplied with the repair kit, turn the lens so that the rear side faces up. Pour the repair material into the hypodermic needle that comes in the kit. Then, inject the material into the broken section through the bulb hole until the section is filled.

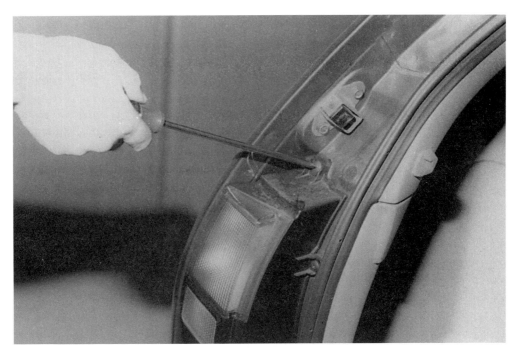

FIGURE 178
Taillight lenses of most makes of cars are held by screws.

6. Let the material harden overnight.
7. Peel off the clear plastic film or clay mold, wash the lens to remove residue, and put it back on the vehicle.

COMPONENT: Radio

PROBLEM: **Power antenna moves sluggishly or doesn't retract**

A power antenna that moves sluggishly or doesn't retract places strain on the motor and cable that drive the antenna. The cable can snap or the motor may burn out, resulting in an extensive and expensive repair.

Since sluggishness and failure to retract are normally the result of dirt that has built up on the antenna mast, the condition is usually easy to rectify by following this procedure:

1. Turn on the radio so that the antenna mast extends itself.
2. Dampen a clean cloth with mineral spirits or paint thinner and wipe down the antenna mast (Figure 179).
3. Turn off the radio to let the antenna retract.
4. Turn on the radio and again wipe the extended mast with mineral spirits or paint thinner. Repeat the procedure until no dirt appears on the cloth.
5. Dampen a clean cloth with lightweight household oil and wipe the extended antenna mast.
6. Turn off the radio so that the antenna retracts. Then, turn it on again and use a clean cloth to wipe excess oil from the mast.

FIGURE 179
Cleaning a power antenna periodically with a solvent, such as mineral spirits, will usually prevent drive motor and cable failure.

184

COMPONENT: **Radio**

PROBLEM: **Poor reception**

If radio reception fades in and out, or if static is a problem, play a tape or compact disc to determine whether the antenna is at fault or the cause of the trouble lies with the sound system. If reception is now perfect, the trouble lies with the antenna.

A problem with the speakers or amplifier or with a power antenna should be referred to a radio technician. If your car is equipped with a manual antenna, however, poor reception is often the result of a faulty ground. Here is what to do:

1. With the antenna fully extended, wipe the mast with a cloth.
2. Remove the mast from the fender (Figures 180 and 181).
3. Clean corrosion from the antenna threads and from the hole in the fender through which the antenna extends (Figures 182 and 183).
4. Screw the antenna back into the fender.

FIGURE 180
Loosen the antenna.

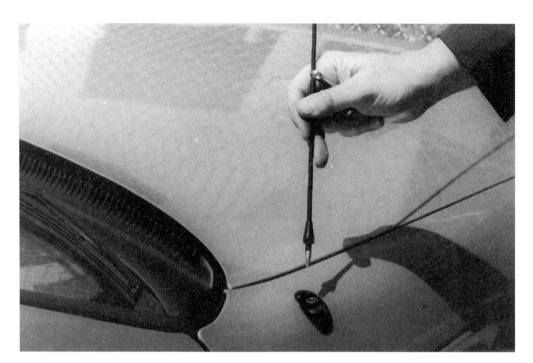

FIGURE 181
Remove the antenna from the fender.

FIGURE 182
Use sandpaper to clean corrosion from the base of the antenna.

FIGURE 183
Clean corrosion from the mounting in the fender.

COMPONENT: **Radio**

PROBLEM: **Popping noises**

During car manufacture, terminals of spark cables are often coated with silicone lubricant. The lubricant prevents the terminals from corroding while a vehicle remains in dealer storage. Before the car is delivered to the customer, the lubricant is supposed to be wiped off, but many times it isn't. In such cases the lubricant acts as a conductor, transmitting ignition noise to the radio in the form of popping sounds.

Here is what to do before consulting a radio technician:

1. With the engine turned off, grasp the end of a spark plug cable at the distributor. Twist and pull until the cable comes free.
2. Insert a wedge of cloth into the boot over the terminal and wipe the terminal. Then, insert the cloth into the tower of the distributor and wipe that clean also.
3. Press the cable terminal into the distributor tower, making certain that it is fully seated, and proceed to the next cable until all are treated.

Another source of radio noise could be the rotor inside the distributor, which also may have been coated with lubricant. Remove the distributor cap and wipe off the rotor, especially the metal pickup terminal. Then, put the cap back on the distributor.

COMPONENT: **Steering wheel**

PROBLEM: **Squeak from a tilt wheel**

If a squeak is heard when turning a tilt steering wheel, the elbow joint of the tilt mechanism probably requires lubrication. Use Lubriplate Spray-Lube™ or similar products sold in auto supply stores.

Start the engine and let it run at idle speed. Place the steering wheel in its fully upright position. As you turn the steering wheel all the way to the left and then all the way to the right one time only, squirt lubricant into the tilt-release lever housing (Figure 184).

Hold the tilt-release lever in the release position and move the steering wheel fully up and down about 10 times to spread the lubricant (Figure 185). If you still get a squeak, repeat the treatment.

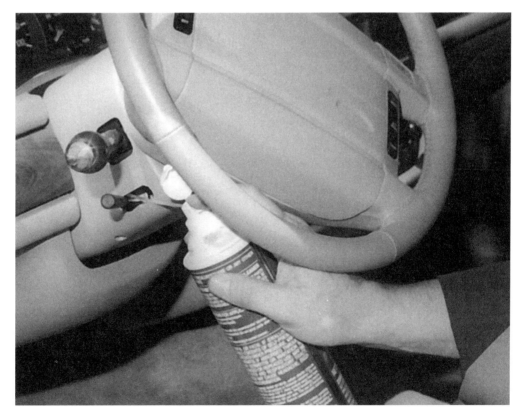

FIGURE 184
Squirt lubricant into the tilt steering wheel release-lever housing.

FIGURE 185
Move the steering wheel up and down to spread the lubricant.

COMPONENT: **Suspension system**

PROBLEM: **Vehicle bounces and shimmies when driving over bumps**

Most vehicles are equipped with a conventional shock absorber at each corner or with a MacPherson strut shock absorber in each front corner and a conventional shock absorber in each rear corner.

A conventional shock absorber is a fluid-filled sealed chamber that is separate from the coil spring with which it works. A MacPherson strut shock absorber is a fluid-filled sealed chamber that is combined into an assembly with its coil spring (Figure 186). Unless designated otherwise,

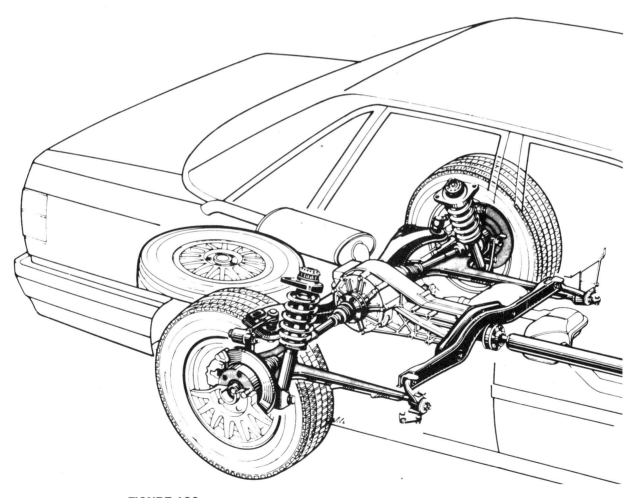

FIGURE 186
A MacPherson strut has the shock absorber and coil spring together as an assembly.

the term "shock absorber" is used here to apply to both conventional and MacPherson strut shock absorbers.

Despite the term, a shock absorber does not absorb shocks transmitted to a vehicle as it negotiates defects and obstacles such as potholes and railroad tracks. Absorbing road shock is the task of the coil springs.

The job of shock absorbers is to counteract the action of springs. If it weren't for shock absorbers, the vehicle would continue to bounce as long as springs compressed and recoiled.

Coil springs seldom fail. The same can't be said of shock absorbers. With vehicles that have been driven 25,000 miles or more, the main reason for bounce and shimmy when going over bumps is failure by one or more shock absorbers.

Indiscriminately replacing shocks without some evidence of failure, however, is not a wise course of action. You could be barking up the wrong tree and incur an unnecessary expense, because shimmy and bounce can also be caused by a worn or damaged component in the steering or suspension system, by misalignment, or by unbalanced wheel assemblies.

Here is how to find out whether your problem is caused by damaged shock absorbers:

1. When the vehicle is on a hoist during an engine oil change, inspect each shock absorber for traces of fluid on the case, for dents in the case, and for cracks in each bushing (Figures 187 and 188). Bushings are donut-shaped rubber inserts that support the upper and lower fasteners that hold the shock to the frame of the vehicle.

IMPORTANT

Although only one unit may display damage, replace units in pairs—that is, the two in the front *or* the two in the rear.

---

2. Another way to detect shock absorber failure is to drive over a railroad track crossing at 35 to 45 mph. If the vehicle bounces or shimmies, shocks are probably damaged.

It is not particularly difficult to replace conventional shock absorbers. MacPherson struts are a different matter, as are shock absorbers in vehicles with automatic level control. To prevent damage to the car and possible injury, let a professional technician replace these for you.

FIGURE 187
Signs that shock absorber failure has taken place include traces of fluid on the case and dents in the case.

FIGURE 188
A cracked bushing is another indication of shock absorber failure.

If you decide to try your hand at replacing conventional shock absorbers, be aware that you will be working under a raised car. If you do not have the equipment mentioned below to securely support the vehicle, do not proceed.

Conventional shock absorbers in the front and conventional shock absorbers in the rear are removed from the vehicle differently.

Working in the front, with all wheels still on the ground, look in the engine compartment to determine whether the tops of the shock absorbers are to be loosened from that position (Figure 189). If dust shields are inserted into access holes cut into the fenders, pry off the shields to reach the fasteners that secure the tops of the shock absorbers to the vehicle. If the tops of front shock absorbers can't be reached through the engine compartment, then they are designed to be loosened from under the car.

With an automatic transmission in Park or a manual transmission in gear, and with the parking brake securely engaged, raise the front of the car, place jack stands under the lower suspension arms, and lower the front of the car squarely onto the jack stands. Then, place wheel chocks firmly against the rear tires.

FIGURE 189
The upper portions of front shock absorbers in this car are secured to and must be released from the fender.

If you determine that the tops of the shock absorbers are designed to be loosened from under the vehicle, remove the wheel and tire assemblies to see whether you can reach the fasteners through the wheel wells. If the hardware can be removed from inside the engine compartment, after prying off dust shields, loosen and remove the retainer caps that cover the threaded shafts of the shock absorbers. Then, take off the bushings and nuts.

IMPORTANT

There is a good possibility that hardware will be rusted and difficult to loosen. Overcome this problem by applying a lot of penetrating oil to fasteners. Allow oil to work on rust for at least 30 minutes. If more oil is needed, repeat the application.

When the tops of the shock absorbers are free, remove nuts and bolts that are holding the lower parts of shocks to the vehicle (Figure 190).

FIGURE 190
Remove bolts holding the bottom of the shock absorber; then, slide the part off.

Working in the rear, determine whether the top shock absorber mounts are reached from inside the cargo compartment, from under the rear seat (which then must be removed), or from under the vehicle. With an automatic transmission in Park or a manual transmission in gear, and with the parking brake securely engaged, shove chocks against the front tires. Then, raise the back end of the vehicle. Position two jack stands under the rear axle, with each jack stand placed as close as possible to each shock. Lower the vehicle squarely onto the jack stands. Now, following the same steps described above for removing front shock absorbers, remove the rear shock absorbers.

Before installing new shock absorbers, extend and compress the units several times. This is done to expel air, which could interfere with shock absorber action, that may be trapped in a shock absorber tube. When installing new units, make sure that upper and lower fasteners are tightened as much as possible.

COMPONENT: **Tires**

PROBLEM: **Loss of air**

Loss of air in a tire over the course of a few days points to a leaky valve core. To confirm this possibility, remove the valve cap or unscrew the valve extender. Spread a little soapy water over the valve. Bubbling confirms the existence of a slow leak.

You need a special tool to remove and install a tire valve core. This inexpensive tool is available from auto supply stores.

> **NOTE** If you don't have access to an air compressor, drive to a service station and do the repair there so you will have an air supply on hand.

Use the valve core tool to remove the faulty valve core. When all the air is out of the tire, screw in the new valve core and tighten it securely. Then, inflate the tire to the pressure specified in your owner's manual or on the tire decal that is attached to the vehicle, usually on the driver-side door. Screw on the valve cap or valve extender.

197

COMPONENT: **Tires**

PROBLEM: **Difficulty changing a flat**

If you rely on the single-handle lug wrench supplied by car manufacturers, which often can't provide the leverage needed to loosen lug nuts when a tire goes flat, this tip may be a blessing. Lug nuts that are too tight usually have been tightened with an impact wrench.

To save the expense of calling a tow truck, keep a box wrench in your vehicle alongside the lug wrench. If you get a flat, here's what to do:

1. Remove the wheel cover.
2. Loosen lug nuts by slipping the end of the box wrench over the handle of the lug wrench. Pull up on the handle of the lug wrench as you push the box wrench against the lug wrench to break lug nuts free.
3. Jack up the car.
4. Remove the lug nuts, take off the flat tire, and put on the spare.
5. Screw on the lug nuts and tighten them with the lug wrench.
6. Lower the vehicle and tighten the lug nuts as much as possible.

COMPONENT: **Wheel covers**

PROBLEM: **Clicking noise**

An annoying rhythmic clicking that seems to be loudest when driving alongside a highway barrier may be caused by a loose wheel cover. To determine whether a wheel cover is making the noise, pry off all the covers and test-drive the vehicle. If you no longer hear clicking, one or more of the covers is at fault. Install one cover at a time and drive the car to establish which needs repair.

To tighten a loose wheel cover, check to see whether the manufacturer's emblem is held to the center of the cover by screws or by flexible clips. Tighten an emblem held by screws with a screwdriver. If the emblem is held by clips, use pliers to press the clips more securely into their slots.

Serrated clips are used to hold covers to wheels. One type of clip is manufactured as an integral part of the cover. Another type uses rivets to hold it to the cover.

To secure clips held by rivets, press the backside of a rivet against a metal support, such as a block of iron or a bench vise, as you hammer the head of the rivet. This will flatten the rivet and tighten the clip.

Clips that are actually part of the wheel cover have a tendency to deform. To straighten them, use needle-nose pliers to bend them in toward the wheel.

You can dent a wheel cover if you install it improperly. Don't use a hammer, lug wrench, or any other metal tool to bang the cover. Instead, position the cover against the wheel so that clips are aligned with the wheel rim and rap the cover with the palm of your hand. If this doesn't work, use a rubber mallet.

COMPONENT: **Wheel covers**

PROBLEM: **Marred alloy finish**

The finish on alloy wheels often becomes chipped by stones that strike the wheels. When a finish is marred, oxidation can form. Oxidation will also form if a mechanic attaches metallic weights to alloy wheels when balancing wheel-and-tire assemblies. Plastic weights should be used on alloy wheels.

You can repair a damaged alloy wheel finish as follows:

1. Clean the wheel using an alloy wheel cleaner, such as Westley Wheel Magic™.
2. Remove oxidation with 400-grit sandpaper or a Scotchbrite™ pad.
3. Feather the edges of stone chips in toward the undamaged finish with sandpaper or the pad.
4. Wash the wheel with rubbing alcohol to remove residue.
5. If the alloy wheel is colorless, buy a can of clearcoat paint from a store that sells auto paint. Spread the clearcoat on the areas that were sanded or treated with the Scotchbrite™ pad. If wheels are painted, buy a matching color and use an artist's brush to apply it.

COMPONENT: **Windows**

PROBLEM: **Difficult-to-remove film/haze on interior side**

A film or haze on the interior sides of the windows, which washing does not remove, is caused by smoke, condensation, dust, or vapors given off by plastic and vinyl components. These vapors are called plasticizers.

To treat tough-to-clean glass, use a mixture of ammonia and water. If washing with the solution has little effect, use a pad of No. 0000 steel wool. Spray the glass with a window cleaner and *lightly* rub it with the steel wool pad. Make sure the glass is wet as you do this, or the steel wool may scratch the glass.

CAUTION

Some older vehicles were manufactured with a plastic overlay covering the inside of the windshield that acts as a barrier against flying splinters if glass shatters in an accident. This type of windshield should not be rubbed with steel wool. Check the owner's manual to find out whether your windshield would be affected.

COMPONENT: **Windshield washers**

PROBLEM: **Washers don't work**

If windshield washers fail to work and there is windshield washer fluid in the tank (Figure 191), one or more of the following repairs will be necessary:

1. Remove the cap of the windshield washer fluid tank.
2. Check the screen at the end of the hose attached to the cap to see whether it is clogged and is preventing fluid from getting to the nozzles at the windshield. Clean the screen by sloshing it around in a container of water or by using a toothpick to pick out dirt.
3. Examine the hose between the pump and the spray nozzle to make sure it's not clogged, disconnected, or split (Figure 192).
4. Spray nozzles at the windshield may be clogged. Use a small pin or a thin strand of wire to clean the holes in the nozzles (Figure 193).

FIGURE 191
If windshield washers fail to work, first make certain that there is washer fluid in the tank.

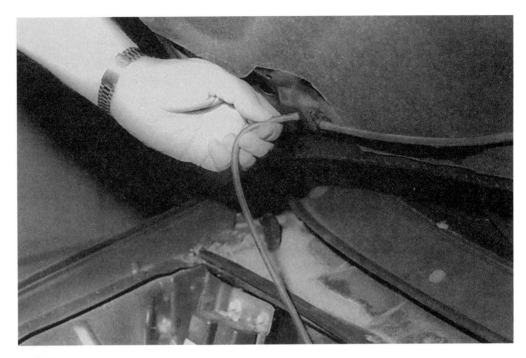

FIGURE 192
Make sure the hose is connected and in sound condition.

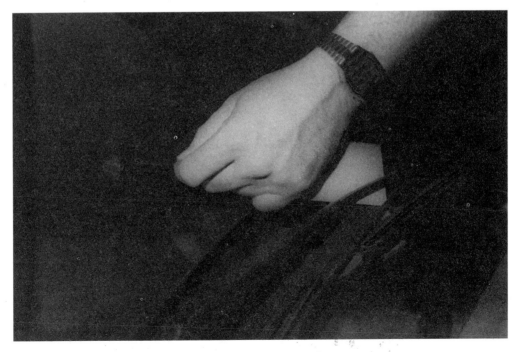

FIGURE 193
Clean spray nozzles using a thin strand of wire.

5. Turn on the ignition switch, but do not start the engine. As an assistant activates the washers, listen at the washer pump. If you don't hear the pump working, it may have burned out. Before replacing it, make certain that electrical connections are uncorroded (Figure 194). Pull the connectors apart and clean the terminals using electrical contact cleaner and a small wire brush. If the pump still doesn't work, replace it.

6. In most vehicles, the pump is held by bolts. Pull apart the electrical connectors and unfasten the bolts to remove the pump (Figure 195).

7. Buy a replacement pump from a dealer who sells your make of vehicle or from an auto parts store, bolt it in place, and reattach the electrical connectors.

FIGURE 194
Pull off the washer pump electrical connectors to examine the terminals.

FIGURE 195
Replace a burned-out windshield washer pump.

COMPONENT: **Windshield wiper blades**

PROBLEM: **Chatter**

When windshield wiper blades chatter as they sweep across a windshield, the fault may not lie with the blades. Wax deposited on the windshield at car wash establishments will cause perfectly sound blades to skip along the glass, creating the chatter.

Wash the windshield with a commercial glass cleaner or a mixture of ammonia and water. Then, hose the glass down with water. You will know whether wax has been removed by the way in which water reacts. If it beads on the glass, wax is still present and another washing with cleaner is necessary. If water flows from the glass, wax is gone.

Treat the rubber blades by making a solution of equal parts of water and windshield washer fluid. Draw blades away from the windshield and rub them down with a rag that is saturated with the solution. The final step is to saturate another rag with water and use that to wipe the cleaning solution off the blades.

Index

Octane requirement, 8
Ohmmeter, for testing cooling-fan
   switch, 109–10
Oil, changing, 91–93
Oil level, checking, 87
Oil loss
   defined, 1
   leaking oil pan, 91–93
   and oil-checking method, 87
   and PCV system, 88–90
Oil pan, leaking, 91–93
Overheating
   at high speed only, 98
   coolant, weakened, 99, 102
   cooling-fan switch, faulty, 108–10
   defined, 1
   head gasket, leaking, 111
   radiator, temporary repair for,
      106–7
   radiator cap, faulty, 94
   radiator fins, dirty, 9
   radiator hoses, defective, 95–105
   thermostat, faulty, 10–13
Oxidation, on wheel covers, 200
Oxygen sensor, servicing, 65–69

Paint
   basecoat, 139–40
   chips in, 142–46
   clearcoat, 139–40
   enamel or lacquer nonmetallic, 140
   faded, 139–41
   metallic, 140
   primer, 145, 146
   scratches in, 142–46
   touch-up, 142–44
PCV system. See Positive crankcase
   ventilation (PCV) system
Pickup coil, 122
Ping. See Detonation
Plastic trim, faded, 147
Plugs. See Spark plugs
Polish, 139, 140
Polishing compound, 139, 140, 142
Popular Mechanics, 127
Port fuel-injection. See Multiport fuel-
   injection
Positive crankcase ventilation (PCV)
   system
   dirt trap, 114, 116, 118–19

hose, inspecting, 118, 119
   and oil loss, 88–90
   and rough idle or stalling, 114–19
   servicing, 88–90, 114–19
   valve, inspecting, 116–18
Power antenna, cleaning, 184
Primer, applying, 145, 146
Putty, glazing, 145–46

Radiator. See also Coolant tank;
   Cooling system
   cleaning, 9
   leaking, temporary repair for,
      106–7
Radiator cap, replacing, 94
Radiator hoses
   lower, replacing, 98
   replacing, 98–105
   upper, temporary repair for, 95–97
Radio
   poor reception, 185–87
   popping noises, 188
   power antenna, cleaning, 184
Repairs, alphabetical summary of,
   xi–xiv
Rough idle
   carburetor or throttle body bolts,
      loose, 112
   carburetor or throttle body gasket,
      deteriorated, 112–13
   defined, 1
   EGR valve, faulty, 33–41
   EVAP system (charcoal canister),
      damaged, 120–21
   fuel filter, dirty, 61–64
   PCV system, malfunctioning,
      114–19
Rubbing compound, 139, 140
Run-on. See Dieseling
Rust
   caused by blocked drain holes, 150
   on wheel covers, 200
Rust spots, treating, 138

Sag. See Hesitation
Scratches, in paint, 142–46
Sealed-beam headlight, replacing,
   177–81
Shimmy, caused by worn shock
   absorbers, 191–92

Shock absorbers, replacing, 191–96
Slipping, of automatic transmission,
   129
Smog, 33
Snorkel (air-filter housing), 25, 26,
   28–29, 30, 31
Spark knock. See Detonation
Spark plug cables
   and radio noise, 188
   replacing, 51–56
Spark plugs
   electrode gap, 20, 23, 24
   feeler gauge, 20, 23, 24
   replacing, 18–24
   types of, 18–19
Specific-gravity rating, of battery
   electrolyte, 76–81
Springs, 191, 192
Squeaks. See also Noise
   from doors, 151
   from loose exhaust system, 151
   from tilt steering wheel, 189–90
Stalling
   delayed, 126
   EVAP system (charcoal canister),
      damaged, 120–21
   PCV system, malfunctioning, 114–19
   in wet weather, 122–26
Starter solenoid switch, testing, 85
Static, radio, 185–87
Steering wheel, tilt, squeaking,
   189–90
Stickers, removing from bumpers and
   body panels, 136
Strut, MacPherson. See MacPherson
   strut
Stumble. See Hesitation
Sulfuric acid. See Electrolyte
Surging
   defined, 1
   oxygen sensor, malfunctioning,
      65–69
Suspension system, worn, 191–96
Switches. See Cooling-fan switch;
   Heat-sensing switch; Starter
   solenoid switch

Taillight
   broken lens, 182–83
   replacing bulb, 182